Highlights™

The Big Fun
First Grade
Workbook

For information about permission to reproduce selections from this book,
please contact permissions@highlights.com.

Published by Highlights for Children • P.O. Box 18201 • Columbus, Ohio 43218-0201
ISBN: 978-1-62979-864-6
Printed in the United States of America
First edition
10 9 8 7 6 5 4 3 2

Consulting Editor: Tracey Dils
Project Editors: Michelle Budzilowicz and Corrie Thompson
Art Direction: Sequel Creative

It's Time for Big Fun!

The pages of this book are filled with educational activities to help your child get ready for success in first grade. With colorful artwork and interesting games and puzzles to explore, your child will spend countless hours learning important school-success skills—recognizing vowels and consonants, understanding sight words, building vocabulary, reading and writing, as well as learning early math and science concepts—all while having fun. With these simple suggestions for making the most out of the activities in this book, you can play an important role in helping your child get ready for school.

1 Find the right time.
Your first grader may be tired or cranky when she gets home from school, so you may not want to introduce a new activity from this book then. Your child may be more able to give you her full attention after dinner or on the weekend when she is well fed and rested.

2 Let your child take the lead.
There is no start or finish to this book, so let your child select the activities that interest him most. If he is eager to keep going, encourage him to do so, but don't pressure him to complete a certain number of pages or even finish an activity. Instead, allow him to come back to it when he's ready.

3 Set a good example.
Show your child the value of work by sitting with her and doing some of your own work while she works on the activities. This way, you'll be right there to guide her if she needs it.

4 Pour on the praise.
When your child completes a puzzle, acknowledge his efforts immediately and enthusiastically. He'll love that you're excited, and he'll be happy about his efforts and actions.

5 Encourage cooperation and teamwork.
If you see your child struggling with a concept, offer to work together as a team. For example, if she's stumped to find more objects that begin with a certain letter, offer up the next one and then ask her to find one. Give her clues if you like, but don't provide answers for her.

Contents

Warm-Up

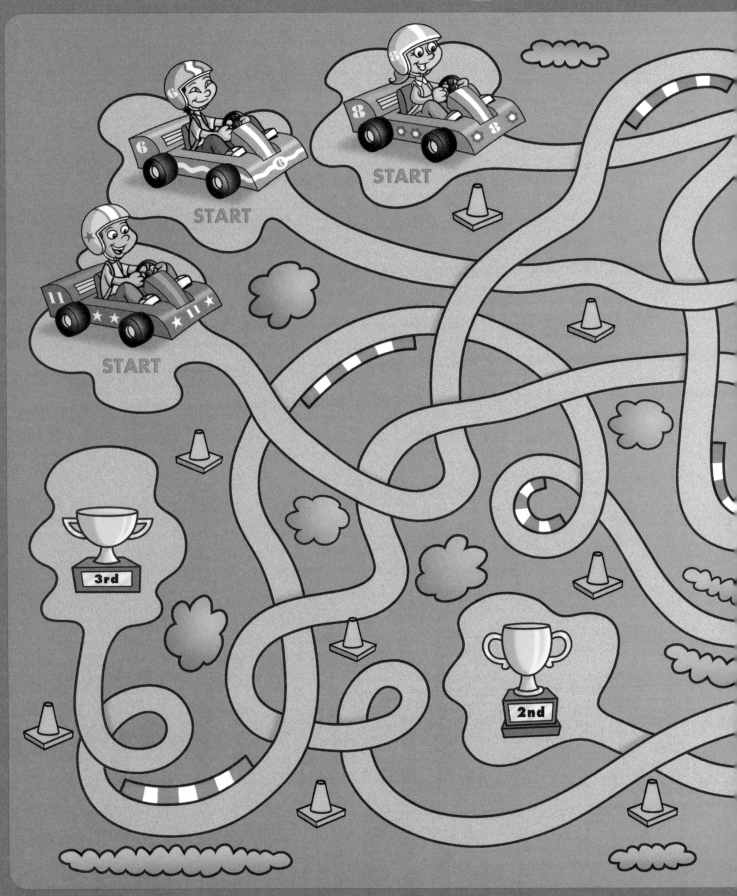

Follow the paths to see who finishes first, second, and third.

Alphabet Warm-Up

Help the frog cross the pond by following the letters in order from A to Z.

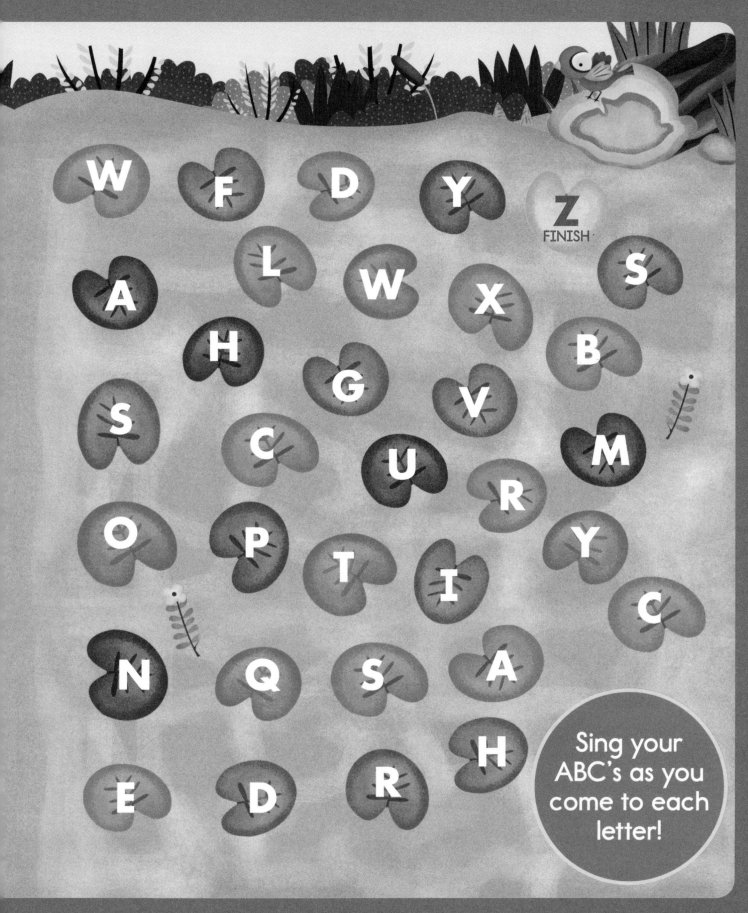

Sing your ABC's as you come to each letter!

Aa

Trace and write uppercase A and lowercase a.

Trace this tongue twister. See if you can say it five times, fast!

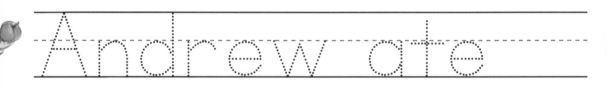

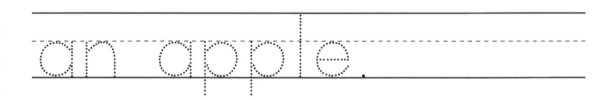

Write a to complete the words.

___lligator

___pple

___pe

___nt

8

How many A's can you find in this picture? Which of these animals start with the letter A?

Bb

Trace and write uppercase **B** and lowercase **b**.

Bb Bb

Trace this tongue twister. See if you can say it five times, fast!

Bumblebees pick blueberries.

Copy these **b** words and say them aloud.

ball

bear

boat

book

Find the **18** words beginning with the letter **B** hidden in this word search. To find them, look down and across. We found **BLOCKS**. Can you find the rest?

WORD LIST

BACKPACK
BAGEL
BALLOON
BANANA
BANJO
BASEBALL
BATH
BEAR
BEETLE
BIKE
BIRD
BLOCKS
BOAT
BOOK
BREAD
BUBBLE
BUNNY
BUTTERFLY

```
B A C K P A C K M Q
U B X W B A N A N A
B E E T L E B Z B V
B A N J O M O B A B
L R Q X C Z O R G A
E M B I K E K E E L
W V B A S E B A L L
B O A T B I R D Q O
B U T T E R F L Y O
M W H B U N N Y X N
```

Cc

Trace and write uppercase C and lowercase c.

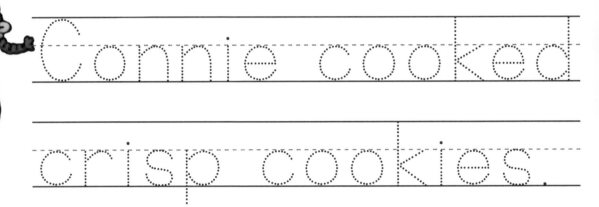

Trace this tongue twister. See if you can say it five times, fast!

Connie cooked

crisp cookies.

Draw a line from each car to its match.

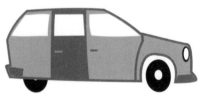

The letter c makes two sounds. Draw a circle around the words with a hard c sound (k) that you hear in the word *cab*. Draw a rectangle around the words with a soft c sound (s) that you hear in the word *cent*. Then copy each word.

cow _____

celery _____

cat _____

carrot _____

city _____

car _____

BONUS! The word *circus* has both a hard c and a soft c sound. Can you figure out which c is which?

circus _____

Dd

Trace and write uppercase **D** and lowercase **d**.

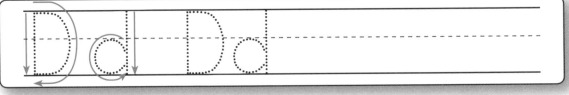

Trace this tongue twister. See if you can say it five times, fast!

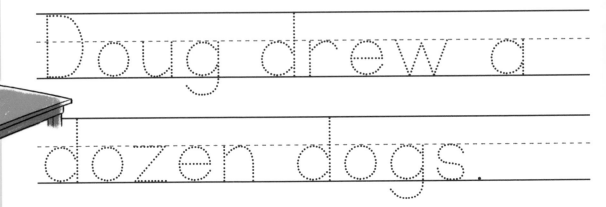

Doug drew a dozen dogs.

Write **d** to complete the words.

_og

_ance

_iamond

_ice

_ig

14

Follow the steps to draw a dog, or draw one from your imagination.

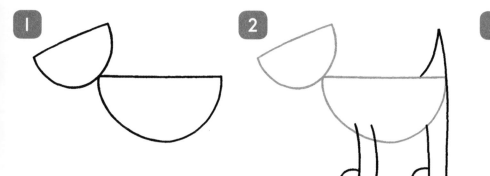

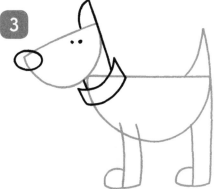

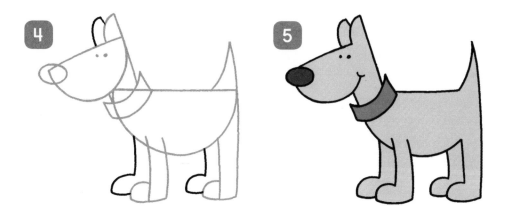

Ee

Trace and write uppercase E and lowercase e.

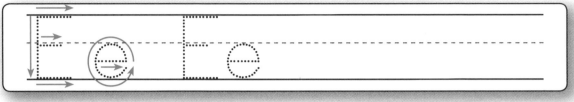

Trace this tongue twister. See if you can say it five times, fast!

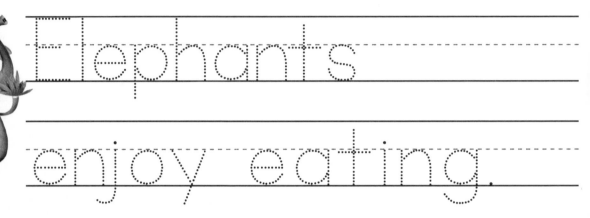

Elephants
enjoy eating.

Trace these words that begin with the letter e, then find them on the next page.

elk   elf

egg   eagle

eel   exit

How many other things can you find that begin with the letter e?

17

Ff

Trace and write uppercase F and lowercase f.

F f Ff

Trace this tongue twister. See if you can say it five times, fast!

Five fun-loving
frogs frolic.

Help this fish find his school.

START   FINISH

Answer the questions below using these words that begin with f.

fin   frog   fish

Who is green and eat flies?

_____

Who swims and lives underwater?

_____

What is on the back of a fish?

_____

Gg

Trace and write uppercase G and lowercase g.

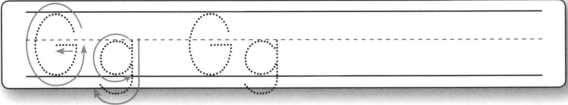

Trace this tongue twister. See if you can say it five times, fast!

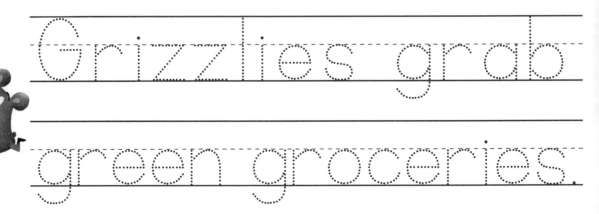

Good golly, there are a lot of G's in these tongue twisters. Draw a rectangle around every G you see. Draw a circle around every g you see. Then try saying each one five times, fast.

Gale's great glass globe glows green.

Great-Grandma Gertie's geese giggle.

Great gray goats graze.

The letter g makes two sounds. Draw a circle around the words with a hard g (g) sound that you hear in the word *girl*. Draw a rectangle around the words with a soft g (j) sound that you hear in the word *gym*. Then copy each word.

giraffe

goose

gorilla

goat

giant panda

goldfish

Hh

Trace and write uppercase H and lowercase h.

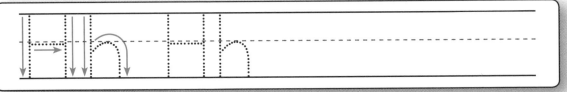

Trace this tongue twister. See if you can say it five times, fast!

Find and circle **8** objects that begin with the letter h in this Hidden Pictures® puzzle.

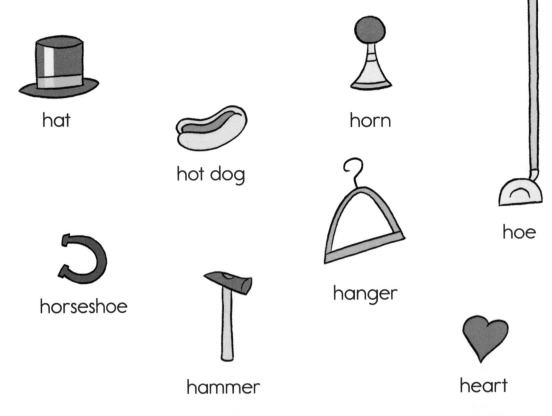

hat

hot dog

horn

hoe

horseshoe

hanger

hammer

heart

Ii

Trace and write uppercase **I** and lowercase **i**.

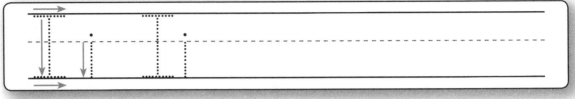

Trace this tongue twister. See if you can say it five times, fast!

I see an icy igloo.

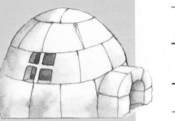

How many **I**'s can you find in this picture?

Draw some ice skaters on this icy pond. What else can you draw that begins with the letter i?

J j

Trace and write uppercase **J** and lowercase **j**.

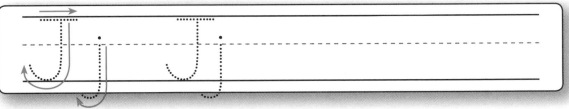

Trace this tongue twister. See if you can say it five times, fast!

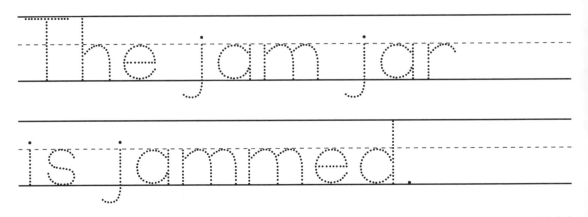

The jam jar
is jammed.

Unjumble these words that start with **j**.

ejt

ceuij

raj

kaject

lejew

26

Help Janet find her way through the jungle to her canoe.

Kk

Trace and write uppercase K and lowercase k.

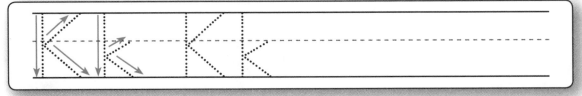

Trace this tongue twister. See if you can say it five times, fast!

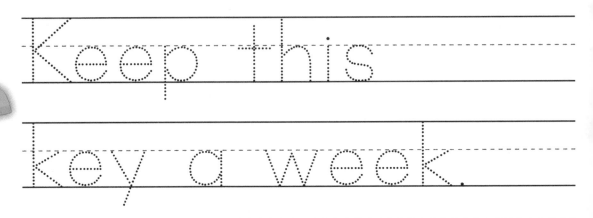

Keep this
key a week.

Find and circle **8** objects hiding in the kangaroos' kitchen in this Hidden Pictures® puzzle. Which hidden object starts with a k? Which hidden objects have a k in their name?

leaf

bird

kite

sock

book

balloon

ice-cream bar

ruler

L l

Trace and write uppercase L and lowercase l.

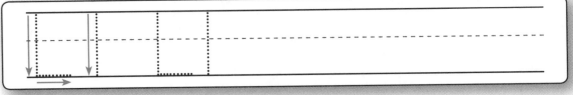

Trace this tongue twister. See if you can say it five times, fast!

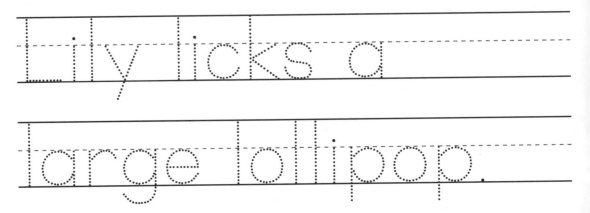

Lily licks a large lollipop.

Draw a line from each leaf to its match.

How many L's can you find in this picture?

Mm

Trace and write uppercase M and lowercase m.

Mm Mm

Trace this tongue twister. See if you can say it five times, fast!

Mike made
more muffins
than Molly.

Trace these words that begin with the letter m, then find them on the next page.

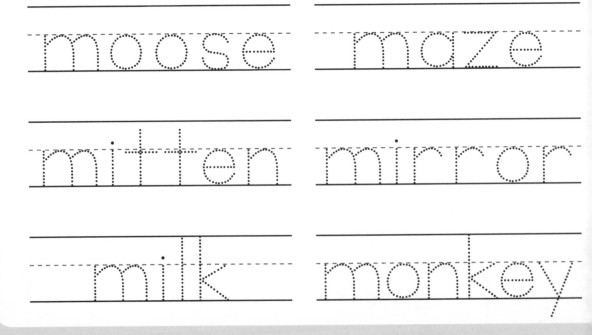

moose   maze

mitten   mirror

milk   monkey

How many other things can you find that begin with the letter m?

Nn

Trace and write uppercase N and lowercase n.

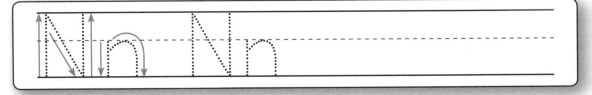

Trace this tongue twister. See if you can say it five times, fast!

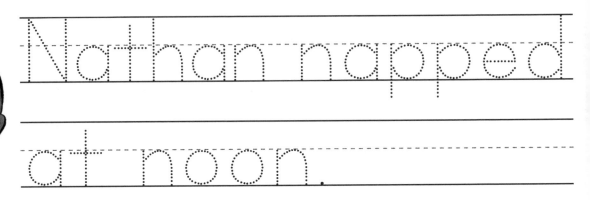

Nathan napped at noon.

Color this newt.

I tried to take a nap today
but couldn't fall asleep.

It seems I'm having too much fun
counting all those sheep.

I count by ones,
by twos, by fives,
and ten by ten by ten.

When I get to
a million sheep,
I want to start again.

Oo

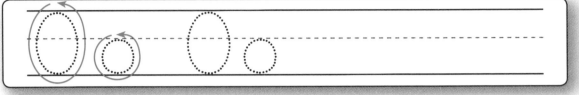

Trace and write uppercase O and lowercase o.

Trace this tongue twister. See if you can say it five times, fast!

Ollie Octopus

opened the

ocean treasure.

Find and circle **8** objects that begin with the letter o in this Hidden Pictures® puzzle.

oar

oilcan

octopus

oboe

olive

octagon

owl

orange

36

Pp

Trace and write uppercase **P** and lowercase **p**.

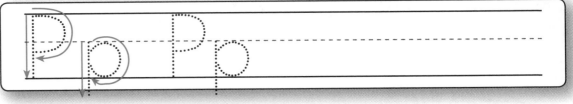

Trace this tongue twister. See if you can say it five times, fast!

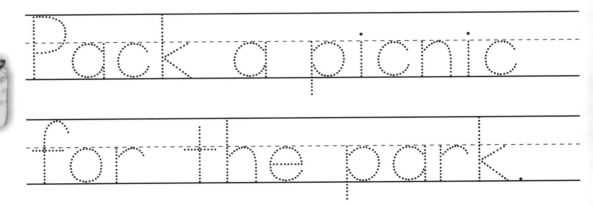

Pack a picnic
for the park.

Hunt for letters as you read this poem. Draw a circle around every **p** you see.

One little pink pig
is sleeping in the sun.
All the other piggies
are having tons of fun.

"Come and play with us!"
the merry piggies say.
But one little pink pig
is sleeping late today!

How many P's can you find in this picture?

Qq

Trace and write uppercase Q and lowercase q.

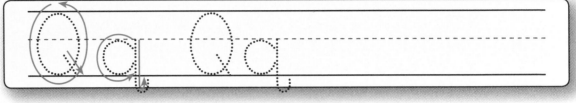

Trace this tongue twister. See if you can say it five times, fast!

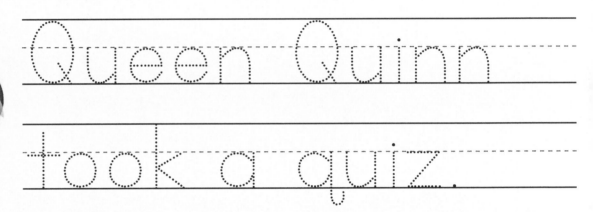

Queen Quinn
took a quiz.

Help Duke Quentin reach Queen Jacqueline.

START

FINISH

Fill in this grid with the **Q** words listed below. We did one to get you started.

WORD LIST

QUIZ
~~QUEEN~~
QUILT
SQUASH
SQUIRT
QUARTER
QUESTION

Rr

Trace and write uppercase **R** and lowercase **r**.

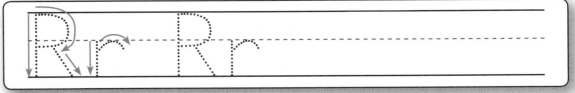

Trace this tongue twister. See if you can say it five times, fast!

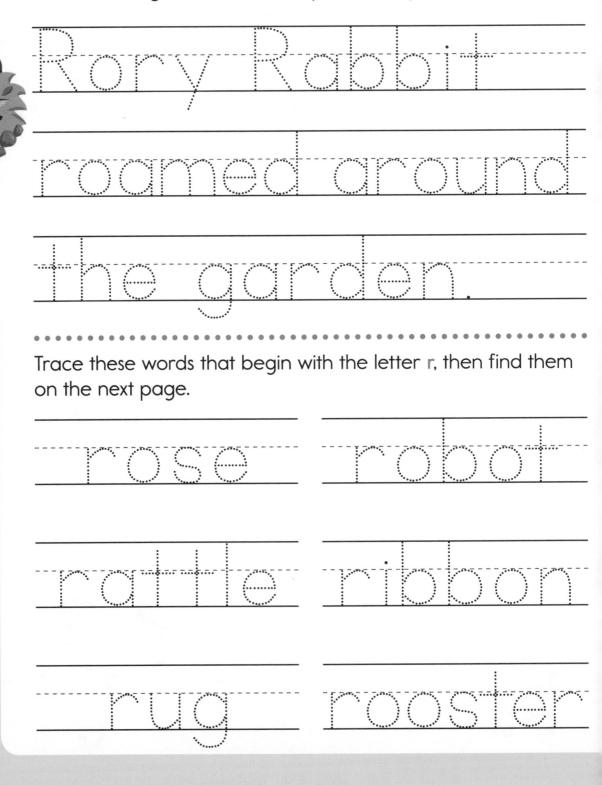

Rory Rabbit
roamed around
the garden.

Trace these words that begin with the letter **r**, then find them on the next page.

rose   robot

rattle   ribbon

rug   rooster

How many other things can you find that begin with the letter r?

Ss

Trace and write uppercase **S** and lowercase **s**.

Ss Ss

Trace this tongue twister. See if you can say it five times, fast!

Scott skis the skinny slopes.

Score! Find your way across the soccer field to the goal.

START

FINISH

44

Find the **18** words beginning with the letter **S** hidden in this word search. To find them, look down and across. We found **SUN**. Can you find the rest?

WORD LIST

SAILBOAT
SALAD
SALT
SANDWICH
SEAL
SEESAW
SHADOW
SHARK
SHEEP
SHOES
SKATE
SLEEP
SMILE
SNAIL
SNOW
SOCCER
STRAWBERRY
~~SUN~~

```
S T R A W B E R R Y
F S S H A D O W Z S
S H A R K S K A T E
A E I S A L A D Z A
N E L N S H O E S L
D P B A X S L E E P
W V O I S O C C E R
I S A L T F J F S X
C X T S M I L E A Q
H S U N X S N O W V
```

45

T t

Trace and write uppercase T and lowercase t.

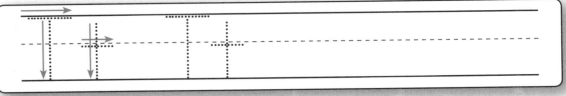

Trace this tongue twister. See if you can say it five times, fast!

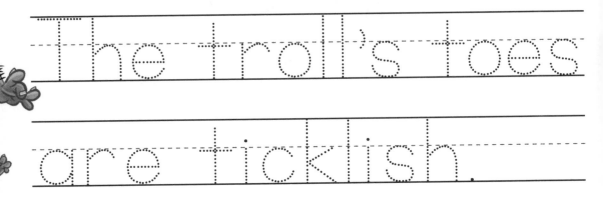

The troll's toes
are ticklish.

Find and circle **15** objects that begin with the letter t in this Hidden Pictures® puzzle.

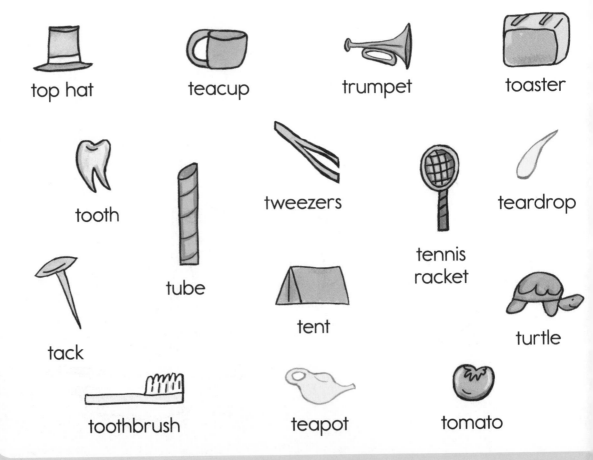

top hat

teacup

trumpet

toaster

tooth

tweezers

teardrop

tube

tennis racket

tent

turtle

tack

toothbrush

teapot

tomato

U u

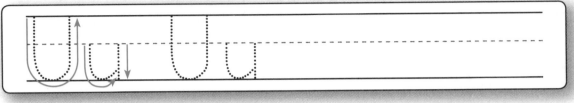

Trace and write uppercase U and lowercase u.

U u U u

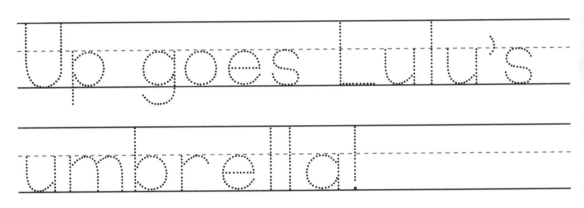

Trace this tongue twister. See if you can say it five times, fast!

Up goes Lulu's umbrella!

Write u to complete the words.

_nicorn

_mbrella

_ncle

_nicycle

48

Use pink to color in each space with the letter U, and use blue to color the other letters. What do you see?

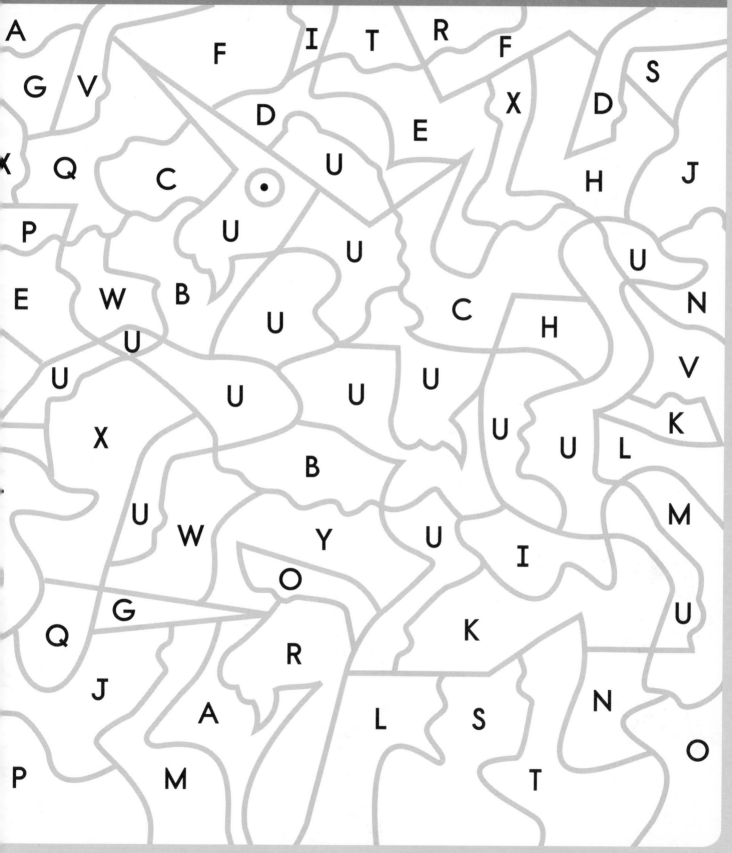

Vv

Trace and write uppercase V and lowercase v.

V v Vv

Trace this tongue twister. See if you can say it five times, fast!

Victor's veggies
are very fresh.

These kids tangled up their Valentine's Day balloons.
Can you figure out whose balloon is whose?

How many V's can you find in this picture?

51

Ww

Trace and write uppercase **W** and lowercase **w**.

Ww w Ww

Trace this tongue twister. See if you can say it five times, fast!

Wally Walrus
washed his
whiskers.

Find and circle **8** objects that begin with the letter **w** in this Hidden Pictures® puzzle.

waffle

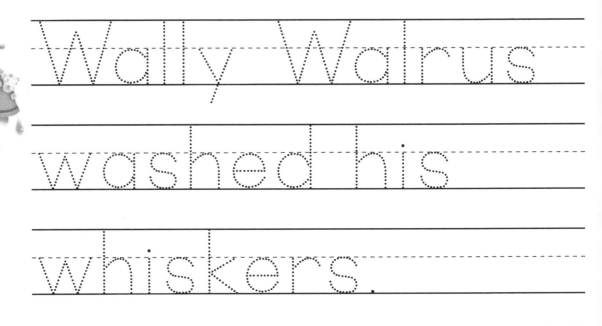

wooden
spoon

wishbone

whisk
broom

whistle

window

wristwatch

wagon
wheel

X x

Trace and write uppercase X and lowercase x.

X x   X x

Trace this tongue twister. See if you can say it five times, fast!

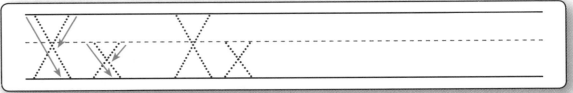

Xavier the fox
mixed flour
from a box.

Write x to complete the words.

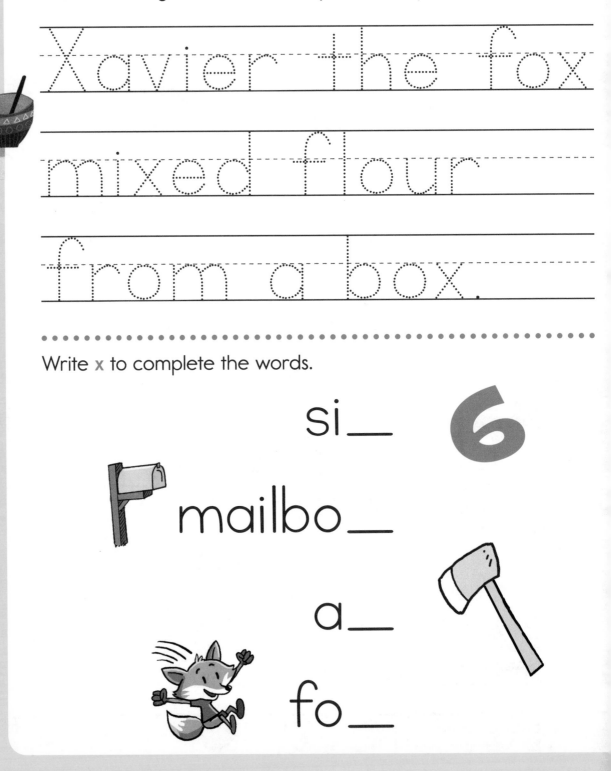

si___

mailbo___

a___

fo___

54

Follow the **X**'s across the X-ray machine to get from START to FINISH.

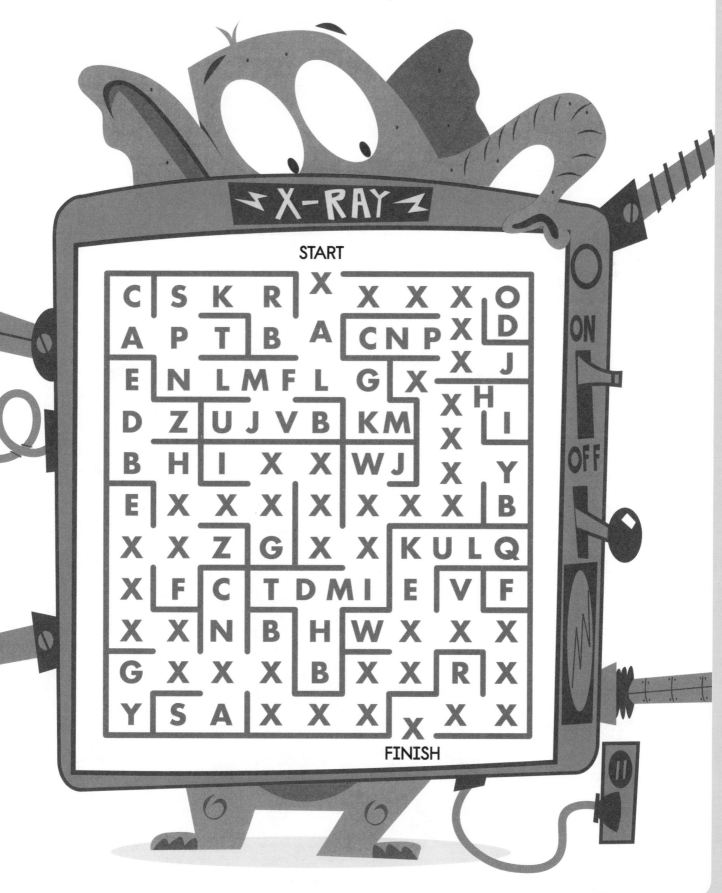

Yy

Trace and write uppercase Y and lowercase y.

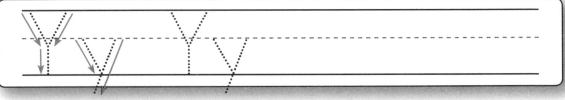

Trace this tongue twister. See if you can say it five times, fast!

Your yak can
yo-yo. Can you?

Follow the yarn to see what Yuri is knitting.

56

Find the **18** words beginning with the letter Y hidden in this word search. To find them, look up, down, across, backward, and diagonally. We found **YAHOO**. Can you find the rest?

WORD LIST

~~YAHOO~~   YAWN   YESTERDAY   YOGURT
YAK   YAY   YET   YOLK
YAM   YEAR   YODEL   YOUNG
YARD   YELLOW   YOGA   YOUR
YARN   YO-YO

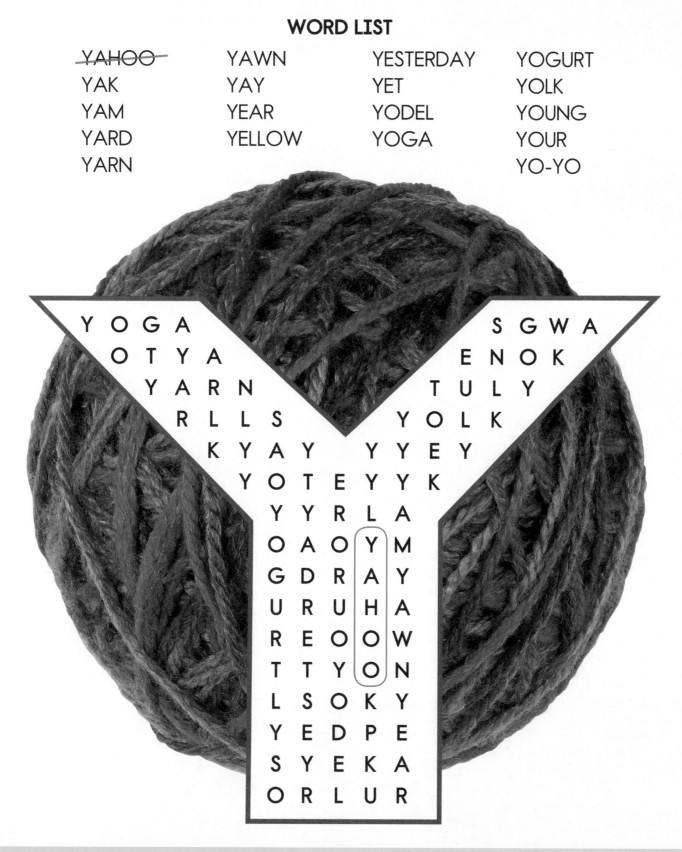

Z z

Trace and write uppercase Z and lowercase z.

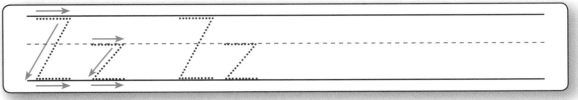

Trace this tongue twister. See if you can say it five times, fast!

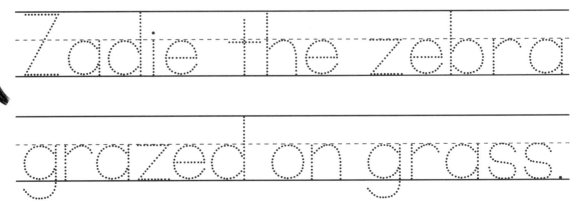

Zadie the zebra
grazed on grass.

It's time for these horses to catch some Z's. How many Z's can you find in this picture?

Zowie! Here are a lot of zany **Z**'s. Fill in this grid with the crazy **Z** words listed below. We did one to get you started.

WORD LIST

ZIP
ZOO
~~BUZZ~~
JAZZ
ZERO
PIZZA
ZEBRA
PUZZLE

Uppercase Letters

Circle the uppercase letter in each group of letters. Then use the letters, in order from left to right, to solve the riddle at the bottom of the page.

L
e   f
r

S
g
t
h

i
u
m   O

T
r   d
k

What do you call a lion at the North Pole?

___ ___ ___

Circle the uppercase letter in each group of letters. Then use the letters, in order from left to right, to solve the riddle at the bottom of the page.

M i r t

c O y u e n O a

z o p Y

t s O k

j q e R

b K r f

Where do cows go on vacation?

____ ____ ____   ____ ____ ____ ____

Lowercase Letters

Circle the lowercase letter in each group of letters. Then use the letters, in order from left to right, to solve the riddle at the bottom of the page.

What did the buffalo say as his son left for school?

" __ __   __ __ __ . "

Circle the lowercase letter in each group of letters. Then use the letters, in order from left to right, to solve the riddle at the bottom of the page.

What do you call a person who serves meals in the ocean?

___ ___ ___   ___ ___ ___ ___ ___

Vowel Fowl

Mama Hen is checking on her chicks, but there are a lot of other chicks in this coop. Her chicks have uppercase vowels on them. Circle which chicks are hers.

A, E, I, O, and U are vowels.

T

C

I

E

U

R

S

W

D

A

O

X

S_y Wh_t?

We accidently left out the lowercase vowels in these words. Can you figure out what they are? What does each group of words have in common?

b_rd

dr_g_nfly

b_tt_rfly

pl_n_

aeiou

- -

p_zz_

b_s_b_ll

wh__l

pl_m

aeiou

Short a

Write the letter **a** to complete these short-vowel words.

c _ t

h _ t

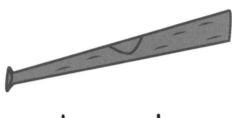

b _ t

m _ p

b _ g

v _ n

Short e

Write the letter e to complete these short-vowel words.

_gg

w_b

b_d

b_ll

p_n

r_d

Short i

Write the letter i to complete these short-vowel words.

z__pper

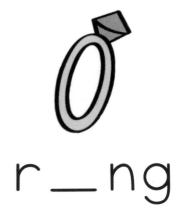

r__ng

f__sh

p__n

p__g

g__ft

Short o

Short o makes the *aw* sound, as in *not*.

Write the letter o to complete these short-vowel words.

f _ _ x

fr _ g

b _ _ x

r _ _ cket

d _ _ g

s _ ck

Short u

Write the letter u to complete these short-vowel words.

b_g

m_g

br_sh

t_b

tr_ck

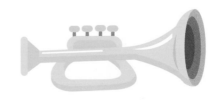

tr_mpet

Long a

Write the letter **a** to complete these long-vowel words.

sn__ke

__corn

sk__te

c__ke

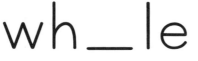

wh__le

pl__ne

Write the letter e to complete these long-vowel words.

thr _ _

b _ _ _

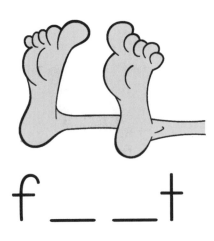

f _ _ t

sh _ _ p

ch _ _ se

tr _ _

Long i

Write the letter i to complete these long-vowel words.

t_me

l_me

b_ke

k_te

sp_der

p_ne

Long o

Write the letter o to complete these long-vowel words.

r_bot

h_me

c_mb

r_se

sn_w

gl_be

Long u makes the *oo* sound, as in *cute*.

Write the letter **u** to complete these long-vowel words.

bl__e

fl__te

r__ler

t__be

m__le

t__ba

Short or Long?

Draw a circle around the long-vowel word in each pairing.
Draw a rectangle around the short-vowel word.

man
mane

What silly
things
do you
see?

pine
pin

COZY DEN
FOR RENT

bat
bait

ruby
rub

find
fin

Consonants

Follow the consonants to help the ant get out of the ant hill.

FINISH

START

78

Beginning Consonants

Write the beginning of each word using the consonants **b**, **d**, or **f**.

__ird

__ook

__ish

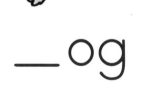

__og

__inosaur

__arm

Beginning Consonants

Write the beginning of each word using the consonants h, j, or k.

_ite

_en

_itten

_am

_et

_orse

Write the beginning of each word using the consonants l, m, n, or p.

__ighthouse

__onkey

__umbers

__ig

__umpkin

__amp

Beginning Consonants

Write the beginning of each word using the consonants q, r, s, or t.

__ing

__eacup

__ueen

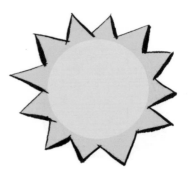

__ooster

__urtles

__un

Write the beginning of each word using the consonants v, w, x, y, or z.

__agon

__arn

__ylophone

__ebra

__egetables

__iolin

Ending Consonants

Write the end of each word using the consonants **b** or **d**.

bul__

wan__

ca__

clu__

bir__

sle__

84

Write the end of each word using the consonants f, g, k, or l.

snai__

fla__

scar__

shove__

sin__

do__

Ending Consonants

Write the end of each word using the consonants m, n, p, or r.

balloo__

swi__

broo__

playe__

mo__

crayo__

Write the end of each word using the consonants s, t, w, or x.

carro__

boa__

scissor__

cactu__

co__

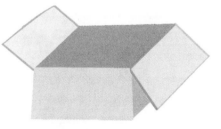

bo__

CH

A digraph is when two side-by-side consonants make one sound.

What words with the digraph ch do you see in the scene below?

The *ch* sound can be heard at the beginning of the word *cheese*.

SH

Write the digraph **sh** to complete these words.

A sneaker or a sandal? ___oe

It says "baa." ___eep

A large fish with sharp teeth __ark

When you're cold you . . . __iver

Wash your hair with . . . __ampoo

You take a bath or a . . . __ower

Not deep __allow

TH

The *th* sound can be heard at the beginning of the word *thorn*.

Write the digraph **th** to complete these words.

wea_ _ _er

_ _ink

_ _eater

_ _umb

pa_ _ _

bro_ _ _er

What happened to the person who stole the queen's chair?

He got throne (thrown) out of court.

90

WH

The *wh* sound can be heard at the beginning of the word *wheat*.

Write the digraph **wh** to complete these words.

_ _ _eel

 _ _ _ale

_ _ _iskers

_ _ _istle

Knock, knock.
Who's there?
Why do owls go.
Why do owls go who?
Because that's how they talk, silly!

PH

The letters *ph*, when put together, sound like the letter *f*. The *ph* sound can be heard at the beginning of the word *photo*.

Write the digraph ph to complete these words.

_ _one

 dol_ _in

ele_ _ant

tro_ _y

micro_ _one

What do you call an elephant in a phone booth?
Stuck

92

S Blends

Match each consonant blend with its ending to complete the word. We matched the first one for you.

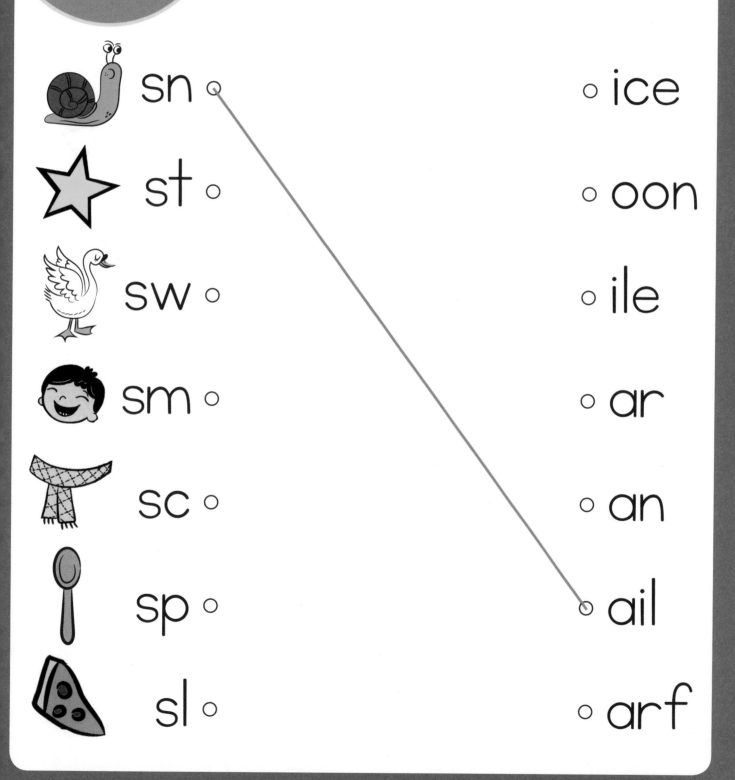

sn ○   ○ ice

st ○   ○ oon

sw ○   ○ ile

sm ○   ○ ar

sc ○   ○ an

sp ○   ○ ail

sl ○   ○ arf

CR

These **cr** words are split between these creepy crawlers. Find the matching bugs and piece together the words on their backs.

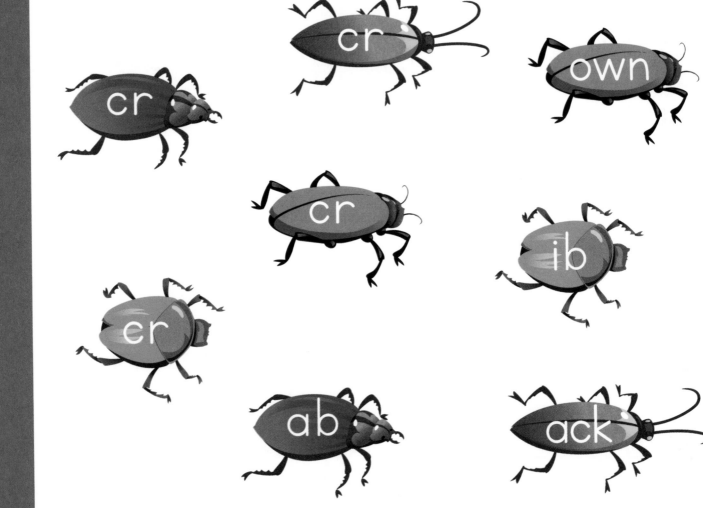

Knock, knock.
Who's there?
Crane.
Crane who?
Crane your neck to see over the hedge.

TR

95

The *tr* sound can be heard at the beginning of the word *trail*.

Write the missing letters in these **tr** words in the spaces below. Use the pictures as hints.

tr _ _ _

tr _ _ _ can

tr _ _ _

tr _ _

tr _ _ _ _ _ _

What has four wheels and flies?
A garbage truck

DR

Drew the dragon is reading these words aloud. Circle the words that have the **dr** sound. Cross out the words that do not have the **dr** sound.

dream

dry

drip

fair

dress

drift

tired

daisy

red

Knock, knock.
Who's there?
Dragon.
Dragon who?
You're dragon (*dragging*) your feet again.

BR and GR

Brianna's grocery list is missing a few letters. Can you write the letters **br** or **gr** in the list to make sure she grabs everything?

_ _ _ ead

_ _ _ anola

_ _ _ ownies

_ _ _ apes

_ _ _ occoli

_ _ _ avy

Knock, knock.
Who's there?
Grub.
Grub who?
Grub (*grab*) hold of my hand and let's get out of here.

Bluebird Playground

Find and circle 15 objects that begin with consonant blends hidden in this Hidden Pictures® puzzle.

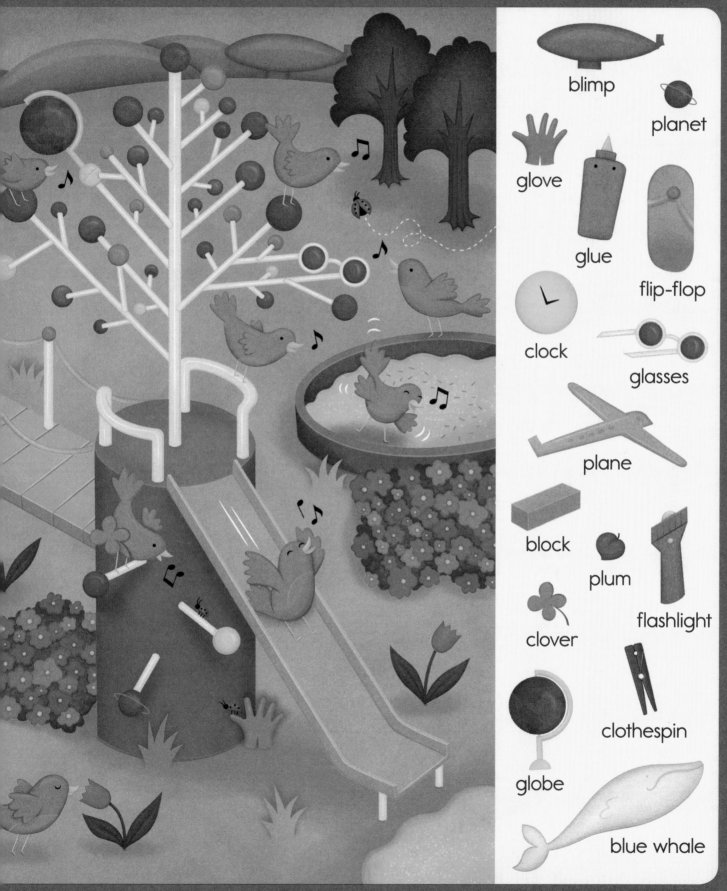

blimp

planet

glove

glue

flip-flop

clock

glasses

plane

block

plum

flashlight

clover

clothespin

globe

blue whale

Sight Words

Complete these sentences using the sight words from the word bank.

I	am	you	my

I __ __ Clara.

This is __ __ room.

__ will clean up.

Will __ __ __ help me find the hidden objects?

Find **5** objects in this Hidden Pictures® puzzle. What do these objects have in common?

seashell

surfboard

sunglasses

flip-flop

tube of sunscreen

Sight Words

Complete these sentences using the sight words from the word bank.

| It | They | He | She | We |

Mark is my brother. ___ is five. Diana is my sister. ____ is seven. ___ like to play cards together. _____ always beat me. ___ is still fun to play.

Complete these sentences using the sight words from the word bank.

him   Her   His   their

This is my friend Bill. ___ hat is blue. His sister Andrea is next to ___. ___ hair is brown. They walk _____ dogs every day.

Nouns

A noun is a person, place, or thing.

Here are some nouns that name people: *girl, boy, father, mother, sister, brother.*

Circle the noun in this group.

man   cooked

stirred   made

Here are some nouns that name places: *park, school, zoo, city, country.*

Circle the noun in this group.

ate   kitchen

drank   smiled

Here are some nouns that name things: *book, television, table, chair, crayon.*

Circle the noun in this group.

mixed   tasted

oven   sang

My Grandpa

Circle each noun in this poem. We found the first one to get you started.

My grandpa scrubs the kitchen sink.

He says that scrubbing helps him think.

So does mixing cookie dough.

And mowing grass. And blowing snow.

What does he think when he works hard

in the kitchen or the yard?

He thinks up stories he can write

and read to me in bed

at night.

Plural Nouns

Write the plural form of the noun in parentheses to complete each sentence. We did the first one to get you started.

__Dolphins__ swim in water. (Dolphin)

We sailed across the seven _____ . (sea)

We use _____ to find our way. (map)

_____ float past us. (Boat)

The _____ like to dive deep. (kid)

We find _____ on the beach. (shell)

There are many _____ . (wave)

Verbs

Complete these sentences using the verbs from the word bank.

plays   jump

ride   sing   draw   paints

The frogs _____ off the log.

Dexter and Dennis _____ with crayons.

Peter the penguin _____ a pineapple.

Oliver and Petunia _____ in the talent show.

Bianca _____ the piano.

The elephants _____ their bikes.

Verbs

Underline each verb in these sentences. We did the first one to get you started.

The pig <u>shouts</u>.

The hippo hums.

The flamingo talks.

The elephant drinks.

The monkey laughs.

The lion leaps.

The ox eats.

The animals dance.

Noun or Verb?

Draw a circle around each noun in these sentences.
Draw a rectangle around each verb.

My mom walks
me to school.

The bell rings.

We build
with blocks.

The teacher
reads a story.

We sing songs.
School is fun!

Palindromes

Palindromes are words that are spelled the same forward and backward, like *mom.*

Wow! These words are racing backward and forward on this track. Find the 14 palindromes hidden in this word search. To find them, look up, down, and across. We found **DAD**. Can you find the rest?

WORD LIST

~~DAD~~
DEED
KAYAK
LEVEL
MOM
NOON
PEEP
POP
RACECAR
RADAR
REDDER
SEES
TOOT
WOW

```
J G Z O C D E E D R
U P O P E M O M E T
Z K F K A Y A K L A
Q Y W T A X A B E F
O S D A D E W V V R
P E R E D D E R E A
E E N O O N L T L D
E S W O W A G T P A
P S Y R A C E C A R
F P V L T O O T R B
```

Compound Words

Compound words are two words joined to form a new word.

Match each set of words to complete a compound word. We matched the first set to make *birdhouse*. Can you find the rest?

 bird

 door

 book

 rain

 cat

 sun

 fire

 worm

 house

 fish

 fly

 flower

 bell

 bow

Homophones

Each silly clue below leads to a pair of homophones. We matched the first pair. Can you find the rest?

A grizzly with no fur o	o Root route
A darling doe o	o Fair fare
A jumbo jet with no decoration o	o Pear pair
Two fruits o	o Bare bear
A story of wagging o	o Plain plane
When the lemonade misses the glass o	o Dear deer
Tunnel through dirt o	o Tail tale
A reasonably priced train ticket o	o Poor pour

Mr. Clampett has heard plenty of excuses from kids who forgot to turn in their homework. Here are some of the silliest excuses he's heard. Circle the correct spelling to complete their excuses.

A World in Rhyme

Find the rhyming words in this poem.

Poodles would twirl noodles.
Cats would dance with bats.
Noses would blow roses
and rats sail off in hats.
Bears would wear long underwear.
Snails would bring the mail.
Hermit crabs would ride in cabs
and whales spout fairy tales.

But then . . .
Kites might bite.
And pink might stink.
Then again . . . maybe not.

Rhyme Time

Use the clues to think of words that rhyme with **chair**. We filled in the first one for you.

What you breathe _____ air _____

It's on your head. _____

To look at someone for a long

time _____

Grizzly or polar _____

A fruit that's round on one

end _____

A shape with four sides _____

"I double _____ you!"

Another word for "rabbit" _____

Rhyme Town

Rhyme Town has opened up its doors. How many things can you find that rhyme? There is a *snake* on a *lake*, a *fox* in a *box*, and more!

Brave Teddy

Read the story and then answer the questions.

When thunder rumbles in
the sky, Teddy doesn't
frown or cry.

And if he tumbles down
the stairs, he smiles to show
he doesn't care.

And if I put him on the
slide, he wants to take
another ride.

But when we go to bed at night,
I have to whisper "It's all right."

He doesn't like the dark,
you see, unless he's
snuggled close to me.

Who is Teddy?

_____

_____

_____

What does Teddy do at the playground?

_____

_____

_____

What helps Teddy when it gets dark?

_____

_____

_____

All About You!

Answer these questions about your home.

What is your address?

_____

_____

What color is your home?

_____

What words describe your home?

_____

What's special about where you live?

_____

_____

_____

More About You!

Answer these questions about yourself.

What makes you laugh?

_____

What do you want to be when you grow up?

_____

Which superpower would you want to have?

_____

What flavor of ice cream would you invent?

_____

If you could be any animal, which animal would you be?

_____

Creative Writing

Answer these questions.

If you could be invisible, what's the first thing you would do?

_____

_____

_____

If you could take a trip anywhere, where would you go?

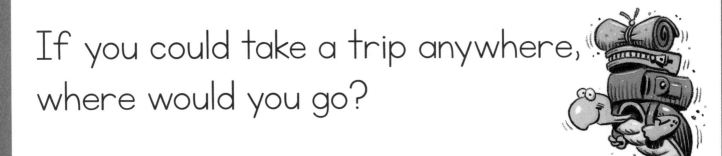

_____

_____

_____

Draw and Describe

Use the space below to draw something you did this week. Then write about why that activity was important.

_____

_____

_____

_____

Finish the Story

Complete this story using nouns and verbs.

Marcus likes to
_____ dinner.
verb

He makes _____
noun

and _____.
noun

He and his family
_____ the
verb

yummy meal. Then

they have _____
noun

for dessert.

Letter Laughs

How are an island and the letter T alike?
They are both in the middle of water.

When is a mailbox like the alphabet?
When it's full of letters

What animal likes letters?
An alpha-bat

What do you call a
person wearing an
alphabet suit?
A letter carrier

Which letter is the
most difficult to
figure out?
Mister E (mystery)

Colors

Write the correct color word beside each crayon.

pink **brown** green red blue
yellow **purple** **black** orange

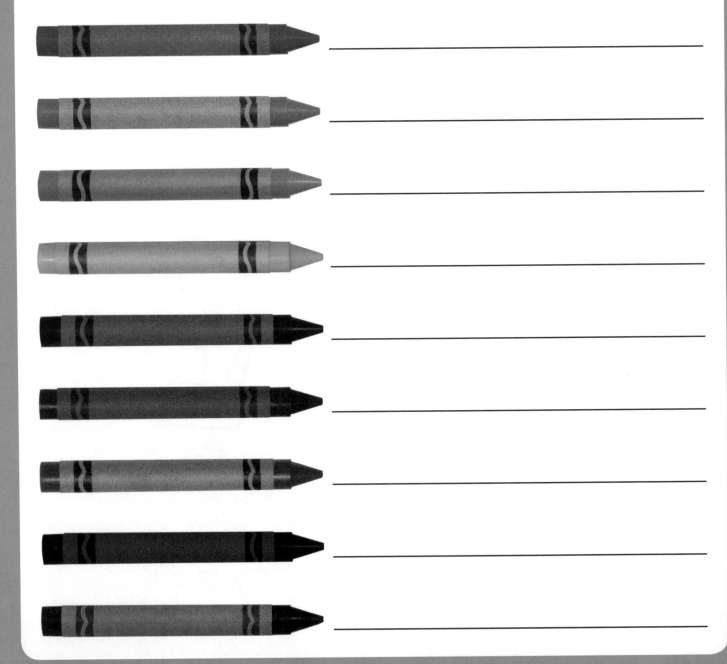

Color Confusion

Find the **15** color words hidden in this word search. To find them, look down and across. We found **BLUE**. Can you find the rest?

WORD LIST

~~BLUE~~
BROWN
GOLD
GREEN
INDIGO
LAVENDER
MAROON
OLIVE
ORANGE
PINK
PURPLE
RED
TEAL
VIOLET
YELLOW

```
R E D G Y E L L O W
M A R O O N Z Z R C
H P B L U E T E A L
V I Z D G R E E N B
I N D I G O Z X G R
O K C P U R P L E O
L A V E N D E R H W
E X O L I V E H C N
T P R X M O G S E W
```

· ·

CHALLENGE YOURSELF!

Look at each word. Say the color of the word, not the word itself.

blue	green	yellow	orange
black	red	purple	yellow
red	orange	black	green
yellow	blue	purple	orange

Find and circle **26** objects in this Hidden Pictures® puzzle. Then answer these questions: How many red hats are there? How many green fish? How many orange shirts? How many blue buckets? What other colors do you see?

saucepan

pitcher

horseshoe

open book

hockey stick

ear of corn

golf club

pumpkin

candle

sock

pliers

coat hanger

baseball bat

slice of pizza

waffle

ring

pencil

rake

boomerang

comb

banana

mitten

envelope

ruler

saltshaker

scarf

Mix It Up!

Rachel's painting yellow petals.
Matt paints blue between.
They look, they bump,
They spill, they jump.
The paint is turning green!

Rachel and Matt used red, yellow, and blue paint. But look at all the colors in their painting!

131

What colors did Rachel and Matt mix to make green?

What colors did they mix to make purple?

What colors did they mix to make orange?

How many colors do you see?

Crayon Find

How many yellow crayons are there? How many purple crayons? How many green crayons? How many blue crayons? How many red crayons? Which crayon color appears the most?

Shapes

Match each shape to its shape word. We did the first one for you. Can you match the rest?

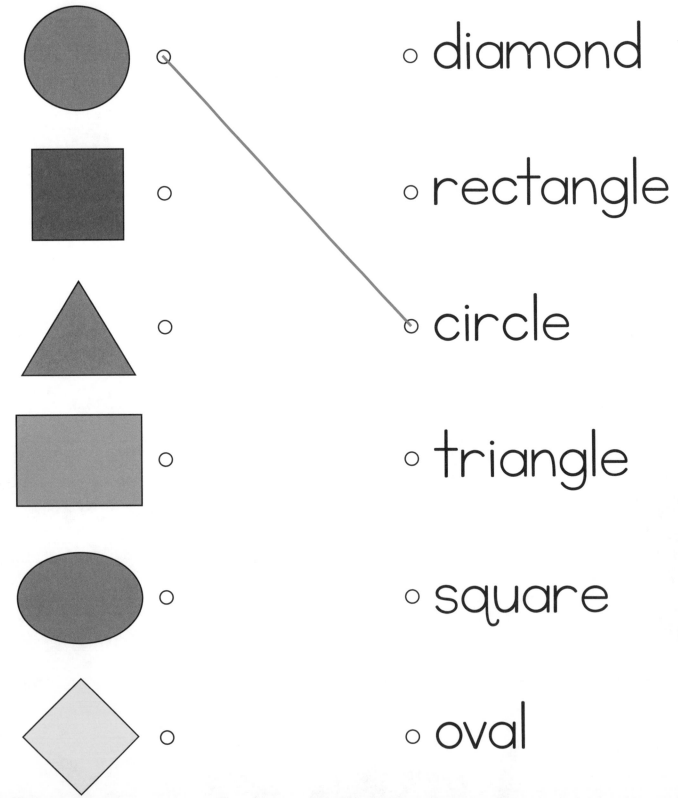

- diamond

- rectangle

- circle

- triangle

- square

- oval

Use the shapes on the left to help you answer these questions.

Draw a square.
How many sides does
a square have?

Draw a circle.
Does a circle have
any corners?

Draw a triangle.
How many sides does
a triangle have?

Draw a rectangle.
How is a rectangle different
from a square?

Draw an oval.
What can you think of that's
shaped like an oval?

Draw a diamond.
How many corners does a
diamond have?

Squares Everywhere

Can you find **8** square-shaped objects in this Hidden Pictures® puzzle?

gift

waffle

window

die

cracker

stamp

toast

belt
buckle

Go Team!

That's a lot of sports equipment! Color in every circle you see.

Sailing Shapes

The sailboats' sails are triangles. How many triangles do you see? The cargo crates on the ships are rectangles. How many rectangles do you see? What other shapes do you see?

Diamond Draw

Color in this diamond-shaped kite.

Which of these kites is shaped like a diamond? Can you think of other things that are shaped like diamonds?

Color by Shape

Color in each space with an oval in it. What do you see?

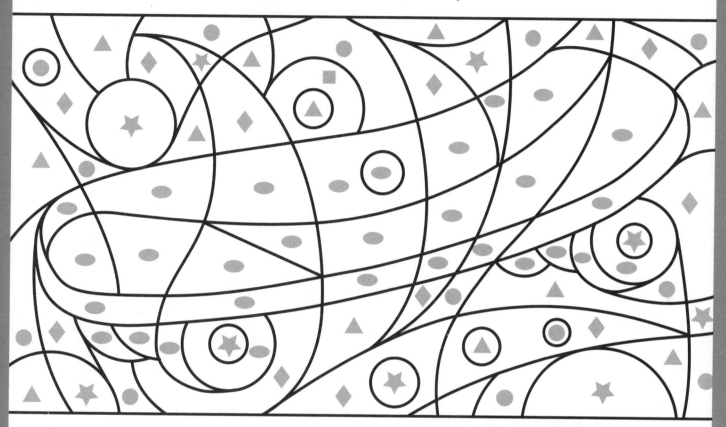

Take time to think about these questions.

1. Can you find 3 circles around you?

2. Which shapes look like the letters of the alphabet?

3. What shapes do you see in nature?

4. What's your favorite shape?

5. What shape do you see the most at home? At school?

Why did the triangle jog around the block?

To get into shape

Shipshape Aquarium

Find and circle **12** shapes in this Hidden Pictures® puzzle.

parallelogram

rectangle

heart

diamond

hexagon

star

pentagon

square

trapezoid

triangle

oval

circle

Numbers 1 to 50

Fill in the missing numbers on these fish.

Count It Up!

How many 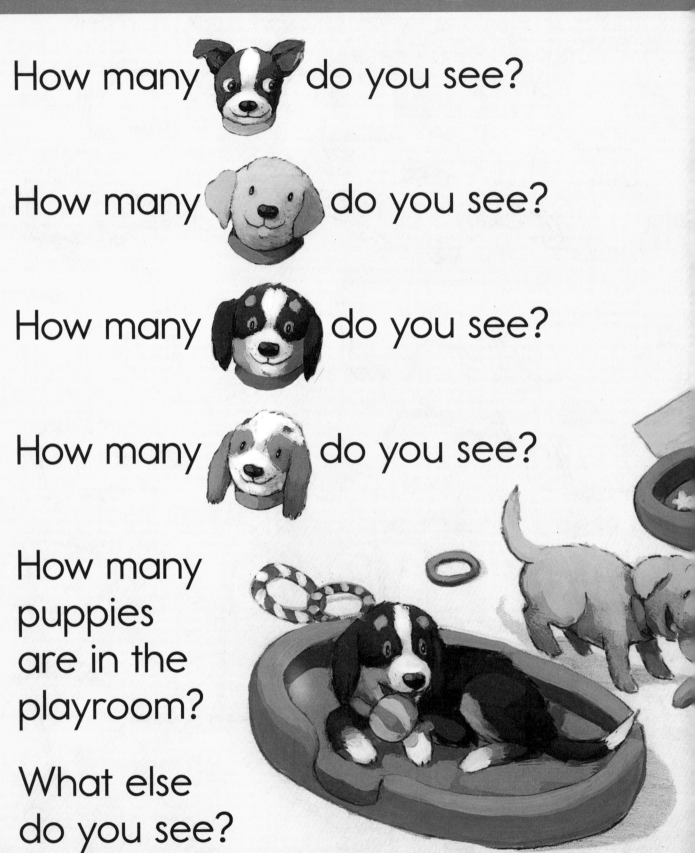 do you see?

How many do you see?

How many do you see?

How many do you see?

How many puppies are in the playroom?

What else do you see?

Counting

Bert is selling balloons at the fair. How many balloons are there in each bunch?

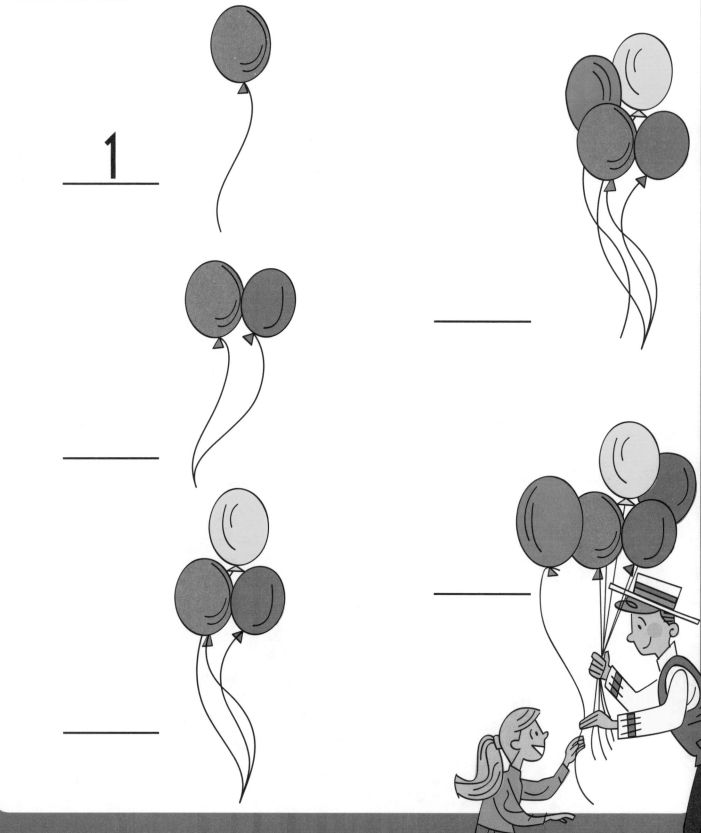

1

____

____

____

____

____

There are lots of bees in the garden. How many bees are there in each swarm?

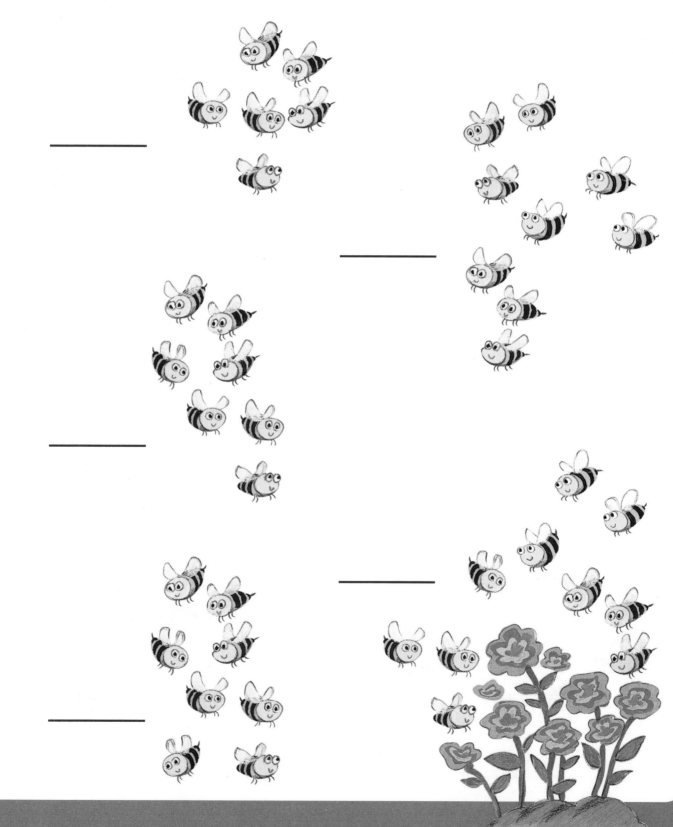

_____

_____

_____

_____

Count It Up!

How many doughnuts are in each group?
Which group has a dozen doughnuts?

_____   _____

_____

_____   _____

How many eggs are there in each group?

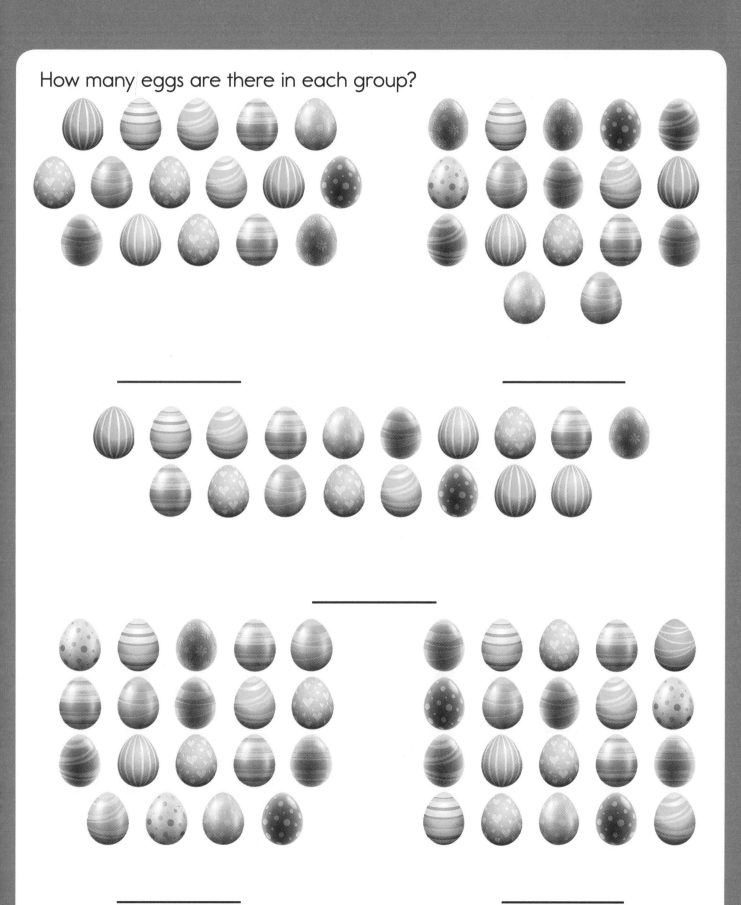

Even and Odd

 If you have 2 socks, there are an even number of socks.

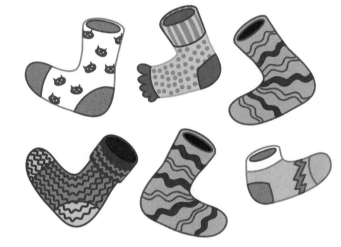

_____

_____

_____

Count up the socks in each group. Write the number. Draw a circle around the even groups of socks. Draw a rectangle around the odd groups of socks.

If you have 3 socks, there are an odd number of socks.

_____

_____

_____

Odd Numbers

Follow the odd numbers to find the path out of the forest. Start at the X and move up, down, left, or right, but not diagonally, to find the exit.

3	2	4	2	9	4	4	8	5
2	7	1	3	5	6	7	6	4
6	5	6	4	6	1	2	9	6
6	1	3	5	8	3	2	1	8
4	9	8	5	X	4	8	7	6
8	2	7	9	8	6	9	2	6
5	2	2	1	6	8	4	7	4
1	4	3	9	2	6	2	5	4
7	6	2	2	6	9	8	6	3

Even Numbers

Even Freddy gets lost in this pond. Help him follow the even numbers to get to the other side. He can hop up, down, left, or right, but not diagonally.

2	2	1	5	6	6	6	6	6
4	6	2	4	8	1	7	3	6
7	6	1	7	10	6	10	13	5
9	8	1	8	5	3	2	9	3
2	4	5	8	4	9	4	6	4
8	1	9	3	2	5	2	3	12
3	6	2	8	6	11	6	5	7

START

FINISH

Skip Counting

Count by 2's to fill in the missing numbers in each row.

2, _____, _____, 8, 10

_____, 4, 6, _____, _____

6, _____, 10, _____, _____

Count by 3's to fill in the missing numbers in each row.

Without moving, can you describe how to jump?

3, 6, _____, 12, _____

_____, _____, 9, _____, 15

6, _____, 12, _____, 18

Skip Counting

Count by 4's to fill in the missing numbers in each row.

4, _____, 12, 16, _____

_____, 8, _____, _____, 20

_____, 12, _____, _____, 24

Count by 5's to fill in the missing numbers in each row.

5, _____, 15, _____, 25

_____, 10, _____, 20, _____

15, 20, _____, _____, 35

Skip Counting

Count by 10's to fill in the missing numbers in each row.

10, _____, 30, _____, _____

_____, 20, _____, 40, 50

60, _____, 80, 90, _____

Can a koala jump higher than a house?

Of course— a house can't jump!

Order in the Court!

Fill in the next number for each pattern.

3, 6, 9, ___   8, 12, 16, ___

2, 4, 6, ___   1, 4, 7, ___

5, 10, 15, ___   2, 6, 10, ___

1, 2, 3, ___   3, 7, 11, ___

6, 9, 12, ___   3, 5, 7, ___

10, 20, 30, ___

Waiting for a Train

How many brown suitcases can you find? How many black suitcases? How many suitcases all together?

How many people are reading? How many people are sitting on benches?

How many trains are in the station? When one train leaves, how many will be left?

How many dogs do you see? How many pigeons do you see?

What could you buy while waiting? How many umbrellas do you see?

Blooming Humor

There are more than flowers growing in this garden. Count the number of petals on each flower. Then write the matching code letter in the center of the flower. Continue to fill in the flowers to find the answer to the riddle.

What did the dog do after he swallowed a firefly?

KEY

3-E	9-K
4-D	10-A
5-I	11-T
6-R	12-B
7-H	13-W
8-G	14-L

Counting Sillies

What silly things do you see?

How many horses can you count in this picture? How many people? How many hats? What else can you count?

HORSE HOEDOWN

Number House

The Numberman family loves numbers. Can you find one 1, two 2's, three 3's, four 4's, five 5's, six 6's, seven 7's, eight 8's, and nine 9's? Hint: All 9's and 6's are right-side up.

Lots of Dots

Follow the numbers in order from 1 to 39. What do you see on the sea?

Most or Fewest

Which school has the most fish?

Which group has the fewest spaceships?

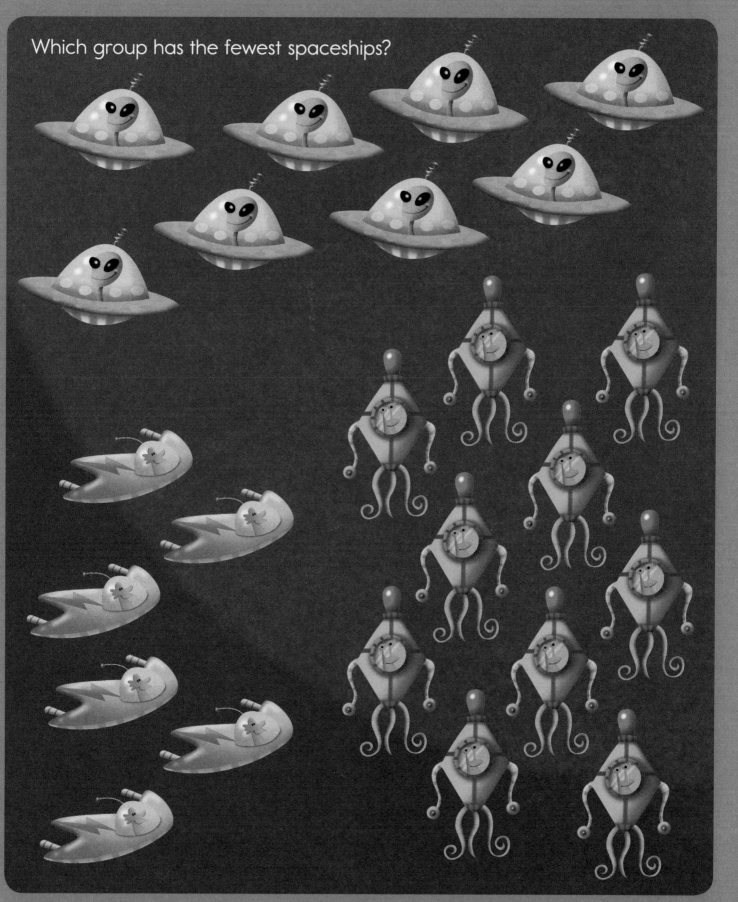

Cupcake Bake-Off

Tanya baked 5 cupcakes.

Sally baked 3 cupcakes.

Color in the boxes to show the number of cupcakes each person baked. Who baked the most cupcakes? Who baked the fewest cupcakes?

Jackson baked 7 cupcakes.

James baked 6 cupcakes.

Dino Measure

Use the rulers to measure each dinosaur. Circle the tallest dinosaur.

Parasaurolophus

Tyrannosaurus rex

Brontosaurus

Triceratops

Use the rulers to measure each dinosaur. Circle the longest dinosaur.

Triceratops

Stegosaurus

Parts of a Whole

Half means that something is divided into two equal parts. Can you color in half of each shape that is split in half?

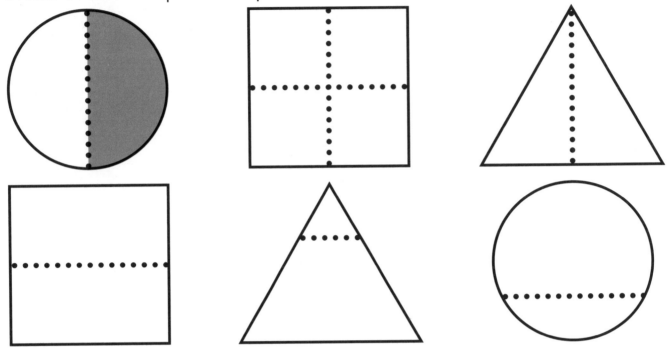

Quarters, or fourths, means that something is divided into four equal parts. Can you color in one quarter of each shape that is split into quarters?

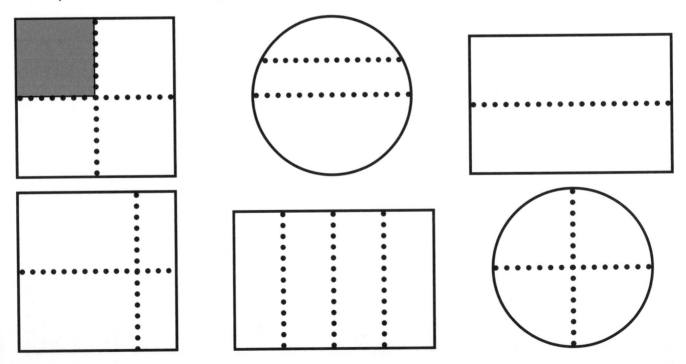

Jessica ate half (½) a pizza. Which pizza shows ½ missing?
Annette ate a quarter (¼) of a pizza. Which pizza shows ¼ missing?

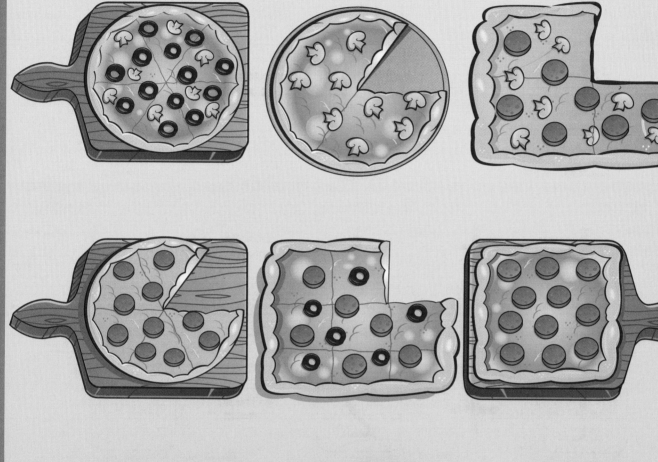

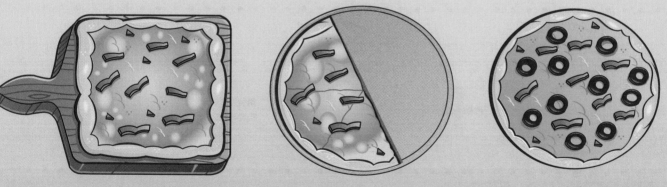

What topping do the pizzas in each row have in common?
For example, the pizzas in the first row all have mushrooms on them.

Add It Up!

Solve these addition problems.

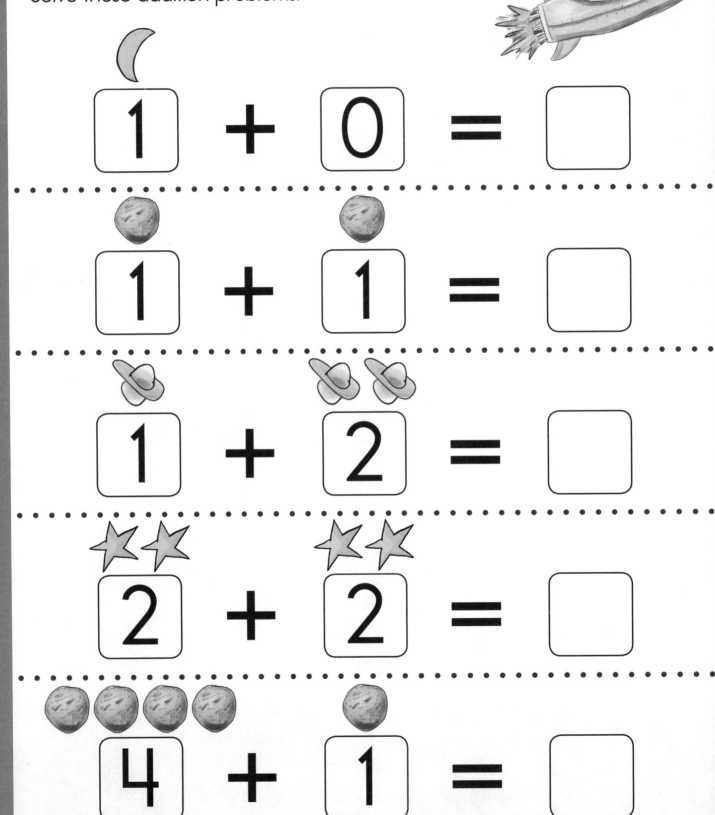

1 + 0 =

1 + 1 =

1 + 2 =

2 + 2 =

4 + 1 =

Solve these addition problems.

What 3 things would you take to the moon with you?

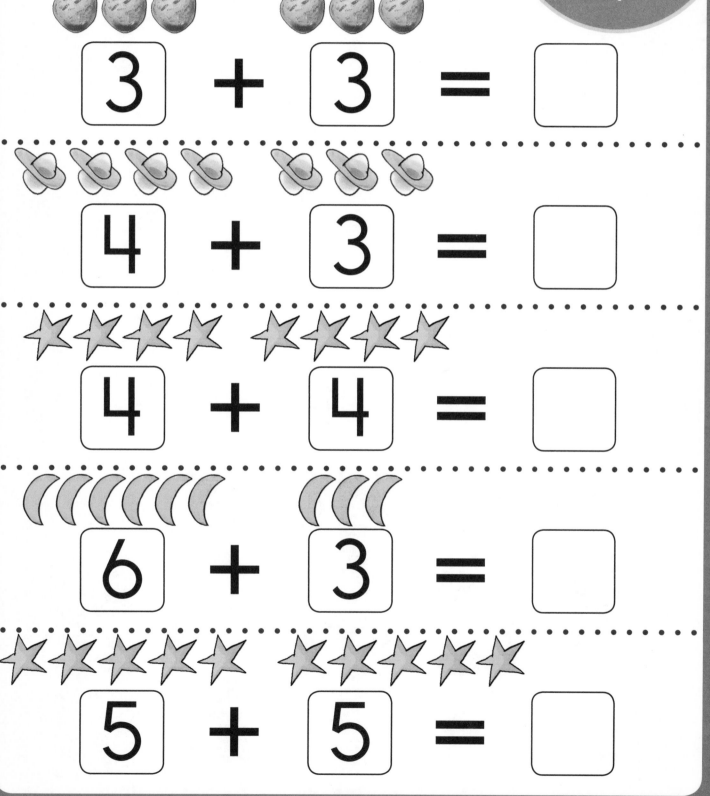

3 + 3 =

4 + 3 =

4 + 4 =

6 + 3 =

5 + 5 =

Add It Up!

Solve these addition problems. Then trace the missing parts of the 5 robots.

$1 + 5 =$ ☐

$2 + 5 =$ ☐

$3 + 5 =$ ☐

$4 + 5 =$ ☐

$5 + 5 =$ ☐

$6 + 5 =$ ☐

$7 + 5 =$ ☐

$8 + 5 =$ ☐

$9 + 5 =$ ☐

$10 + 5 =$ ☐

Solve these addition problems. Then color in the 10 birds.

$1 + 10 = \boxed{}$ $6 + 10 = \boxed{}$

$2 + 10 = \boxed{}$ $7 + 10 = \boxed{}$

$3 + 10 = \boxed{}$ $8 + 10 = \boxed{}$

$4 + 10 = \boxed{}$ $9 + 10 = \boxed{}$

$5 + 10 = \boxed{}$ $10 + 10 = \boxed{}$

Add It Up!

Solve these addition problems.

2 + 0 = ☐

7 + 1 = ☐

9 + 1 = ☐

3 + 1 = ☐

4 + 2 = ☐

8 + 1 = ☐

5 + 1 = ☐

5 + 4 = ☐

5 + 2 = ☐

6 + 1 = ☐

5 + 3 = ☐

3 + 2 = ☐

6 + 2 = ☐

What's a math student's favorite sum?

Summer

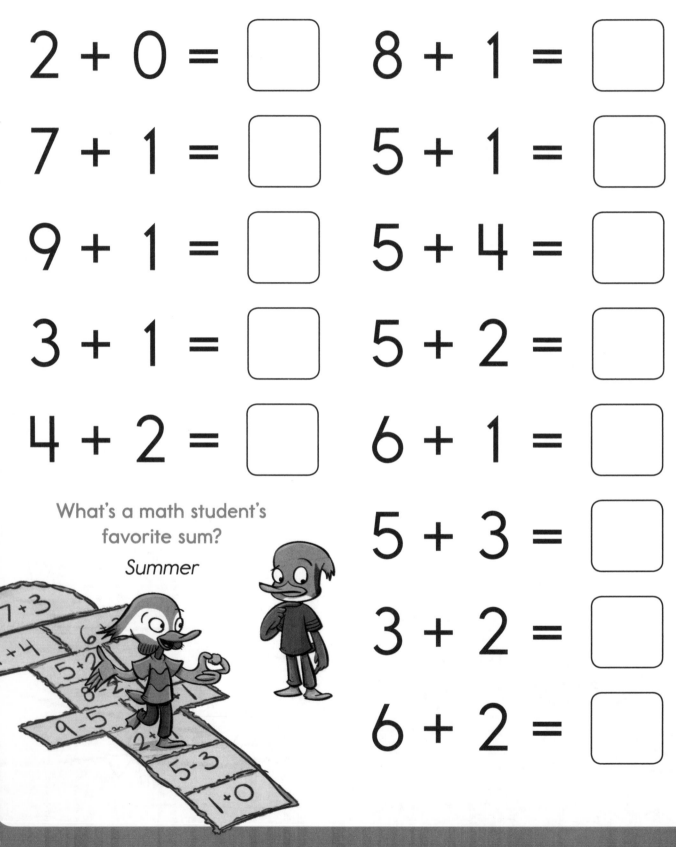

Solve these addition problems.

8 + 4 = ☐   9 + 4 = ☐

10 + 3 = ☐   8 + 5 = ☐

9 + 6 = ☐   7 + 7 = ☐

3 + 9 = ☐   8 + 7 = ☐

6 + 6 = ☐

6 + 5 = ☐

10 + 4 = ☐

7 + 5 = ☐

If you had 27 marbles in one
pocket and 89 in the other,
what would you have?

Heavy pants

Add It Up!

Solve these addition problems. We did the first one for you.

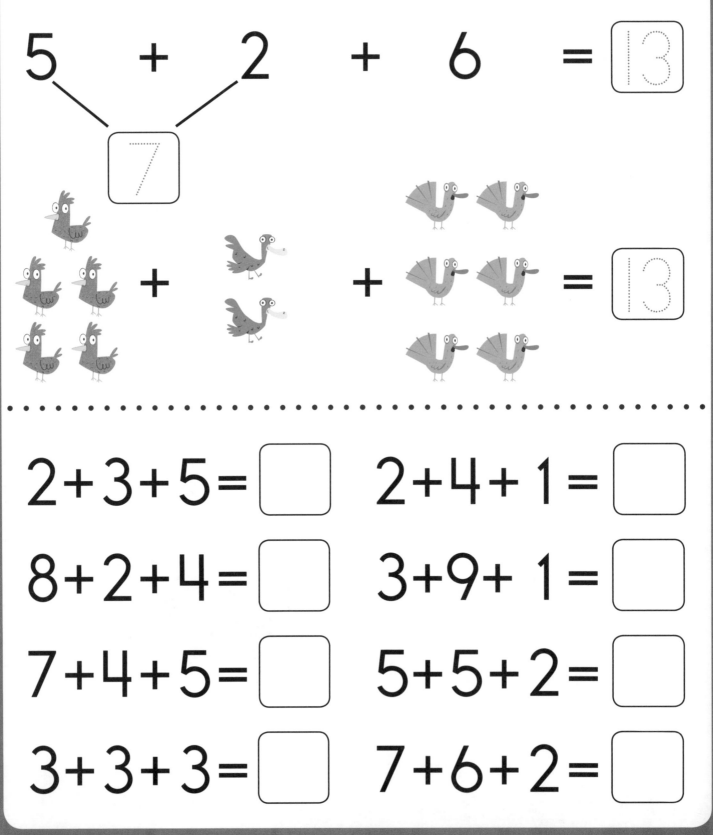

5 + 2 + 6 = 13

7

2+3+5 = ☐   2+4+1 = ☐

8+2+4 = ☐   3+9+1 = ☐

7+4+5 = ☐   5+5+2 = ☐

3+3+3 = ☐   7+6+2 = ☐

Solve these addition problems. We did the first one for you.

10	11	12	13	14
+10	+ 4	+ 6	+ 1	+ 2
20				

15	16	17	18	19
+ 3	+ 4	+ 2	+ 0	+ 1

Why did the math teacher plant numbers?

He could count on them to grow.

Math Maze

To make it from START to FINISH, solve the first addition problem (6+5). Draw a line to the answer (11). Then move to the next pair of numbers and do the same. Answers may be to the left, right, up, or down.

START

6+5　12　8+7　15　4+7　26　6+22　28　4+12

11　14　13　25　16

21+8　29　7+9　17　6+8　14　13+12　21　15+4

26　16　36　23　19

8+14　24　19+4　25　29+7　34　6+4　25　5+15

22　23　13　14　20

10+21　33　13+6　19　8+5　12　3+12　30　17+13

31　17　15　15　32

15+2　28　4+7　6　3+3　26　16+16　13　3+7

17　24　16　32　21

6+3　18　11+2　22　9+1　10　17+7　24　FINISH

Lucky Addition

Solve these addition problems. Place the letters that represent each number in the spaces below to answer the riddle.

$5 + 7 = W$

$6 + 1 = T$

$6 + 4 = L$

$9 + 2 = R$

$2 + 4 = H$

$3 + 6 = E$

What's at the end of a rainbow?

$\underset{7}{\_\_}\ \underset{6}{\_\_}\ \underset{9}{\_\_}$

$\underset{10}{\_\_}\ \underset{9}{\_\_}\ \underset{7}{\_\_}\ \underset{7}{\_\_}\ \underset{9}{\_\_}\ \underset{11}{\_\_}\ \underset{12}{\_\_}$

Reptile Riddle

Some simple addition and the code box will help you solve this riddle. Add the 2 numbers under each space, then fill that space with the letter from the code box that matches the answer.

What do two snakes do after they fight?

___ ___ ___ ___
15+15   12+4   13+11   16+13

___ ___ ___ ___
9+7   20+11   15+3   11+7

___ ___ ___
27+9   11+11   15+12

___ ___ ___ ___
5+20   28+8   20+6   15+9

___ ___ .
5+7   4+24

CODE
12 = U   24 = E   29 = Y
16 = H   25 = M   30 = T
18 = S   26 = K   31 = I
22 = N   27 = D   36 = A
              28 = P

Key Problems

Solve these math problems to answer the riddle. Then find the 5 keys hidden on the island.

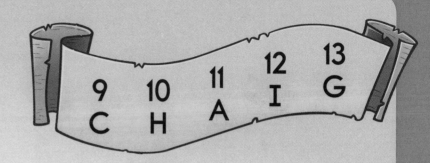

9	10	11	12	13
C	H	A	I	G

What did the pirate get on the test?

___ ___ ___ ___ ___   ___
2 + 9   3 + 7   6 + 6   8 + 5   4 + 6   3 + 6

Subtraction

Solve these subtraction problems.

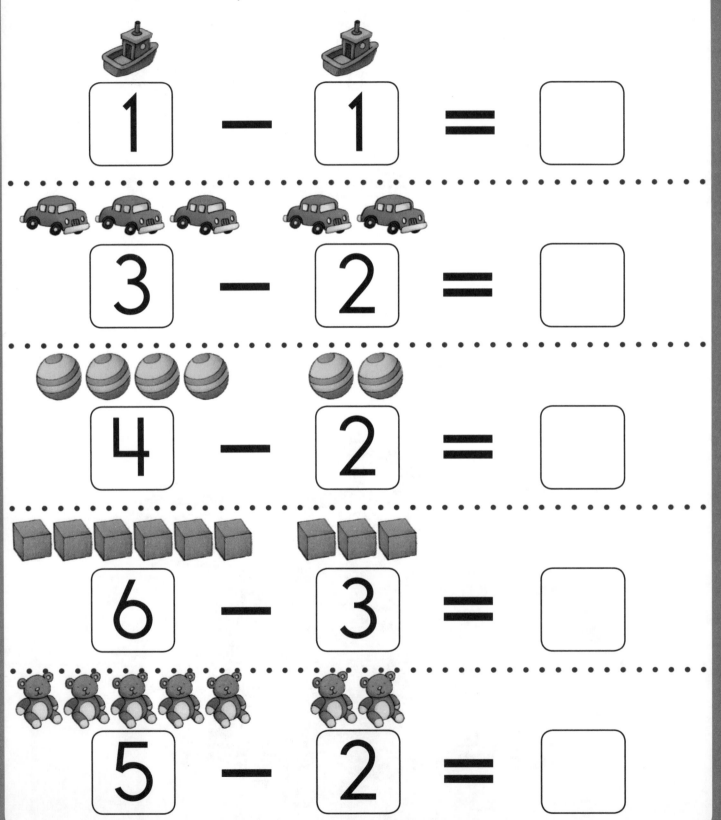

$1 - 1 =$

$3 - 2 =$

$4 - 2 =$

$6 - 3 =$

$5 - 2 =$

Solve these subtraction problems.

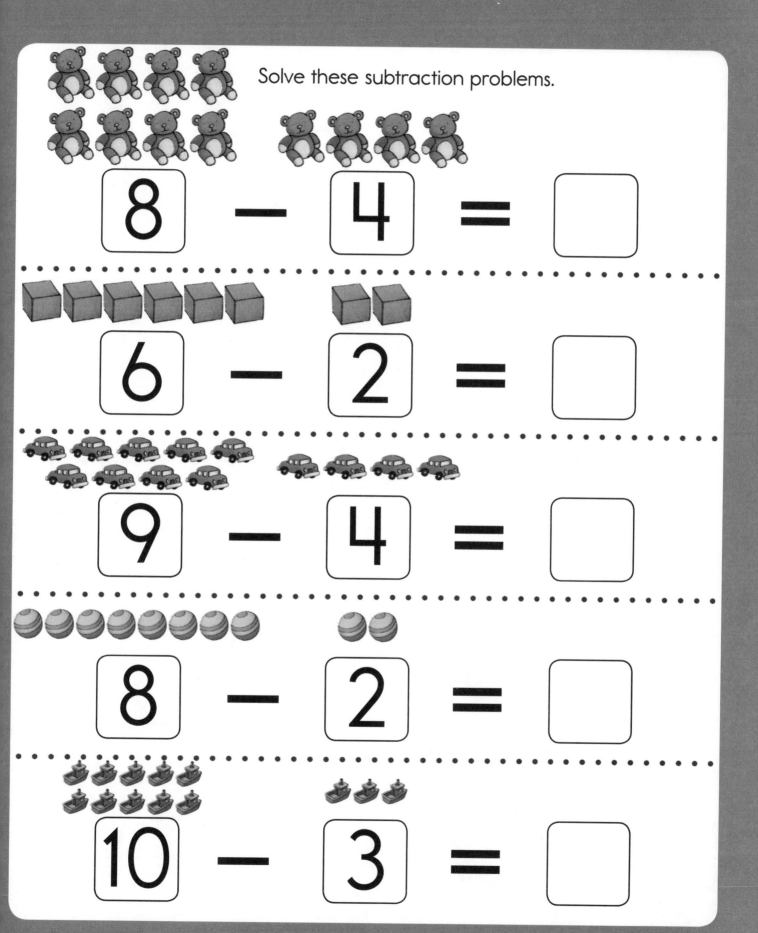

8 − 4 = ☐

6 − 2 = ☐

9 − 4 = ☐

8 − 2 = ☐

10 − 3 = ☐

Subtraction

Solve these subtraction problems. We did the first one for you.

7 – 5 = $\boxed{2}$

6 – 6 = $\boxed{}$

9 – 3 = $\boxed{}$

11 – 10 = $\boxed{}$

9 – 5 = $\boxed{}$

12 – 2 = $\boxed{}$

7 – 4 = $\boxed{}$

13 – 5 = $\boxed{}$

6 – 1 = $\boxed{}$

11 – 4 = $\boxed{}$

15 – 6 = $\boxed{}$

12 – 4 = $\boxed{}$

8 – 6 = $\boxed{}$

Solve these subtraction problems.

7 − 3 = ☐   5 − 2 = ☐

7 − 6 = ☐   8 − 2 = ☐

9 − 4 = ☐   10 − 6 = ☐

11 − 5 = ☐   15 − 5 = ☐

Why is math hard work?

Because you have to carry all of the numerals

Subtraction

Solve these subtraction problems. We did the first one for you.

$$10 - 10 = \boxed{0}$$ $$20 - 10 = \boxed{}$$ $$30 - 10 = \boxed{}$$ $$40 - 10 = \boxed{}$$ $$50 - 10 = \boxed{}$$

$$60 - 10 = \boxed{}$$ $$70 - 10 = \boxed{}$$ $$80 - 10 = \boxed{}$$ $$90 - 10 = \boxed{}$$ $$100 - 10 = \boxed{}$$

$$30 - 20 = \boxed{}$$ $$40 - 30 = \boxed{}$$

Why was 6 afraid of 7?

Because 7 8 9

Solve these subtraction problems.

$$50 - 20 = \boxed{}$$ $$60 - 40 = \boxed{}$$ $$40 - 10 = \boxed{}$$ $$30 - 10 = \boxed{}$$ $$80 - 20 = \boxed{}$$

$$90 - 60 = \boxed{}$$ $$60 - 50 = \boxed{}$$ $$70 - 20 = \boxed{}$$ $$50 - 10 = \boxed{}$$ $$70 - 40 = \boxed{}$$

$$80 - 40 = \boxed{}$$ $$50 - 30 = \boxed{}$$

What did the 0 say to the 8?

"Hey, nice belt!"

Math Maze

To make your way from START to FINISH, solve the first subtraction problem (16-11). Draw a line to the answer (5). Then move to the next pair of numbers and do the same. Answers may be to the left, right, up, or down.

START

16-11	5	13-13	0	26-12	6	16-15	1	23-1
7		6		14		3		5
24-22	6	22-11	3	24-21	4	26-14	12	12-12
2		11		5		6		0
15-3	9	16-13	6	15-2	13	17-11	5	27-23
2		3		0		8		4
2-2	5	25-15	5	24-24	6	18-12	14	23-11
6		10		1		14		12
27-22	7	18-11	0	3-3	16	25-11	13	24-22
5		9		6		8		2
13-2	11	17-7	10	26-25	1	19-11	9	FINISH

194

Sub-track-tion

Solve these subtraction problems. Place the letters that represent each number in the spaces below to answer the riddle.

What do you call a train with a cold?

____ – ____ ____ ____ ____
 1   2   3   4   4

____ ____ ____ ____
 2   3   4   4

____ ____ ____ ____ ____
 5   6   1   7   8

$9 - 4 = T$

$10 - 7 = H$

$13 - 7 = R$

$6 - 2 = O$

$15 - 8 = I$

$8 - 6 = C$

$12 - 11 = A$

$12 - 4 = N$

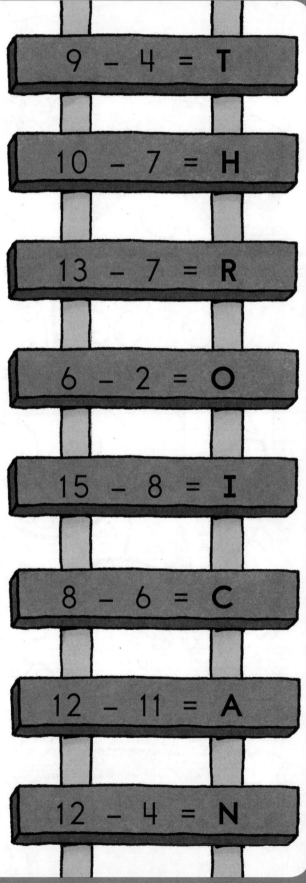

Ocean Explorations

Find and circle **21** objects in this Hidden Pictures® puzzle.

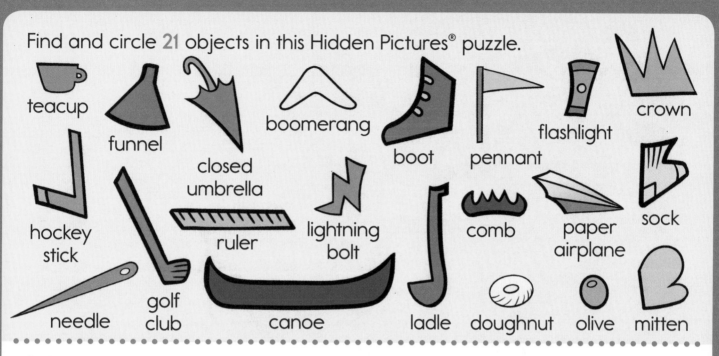

teacup

funnel

closed umbrella

boomerang

boot

pennant

flashlight

crown

hockey stick

ruler

lightning bolt

comb

paper airplane

sock

needle

golf club

canoe

ladle doughnut olive mitten

Solve these problems. Then use the answers to solve the riddle.

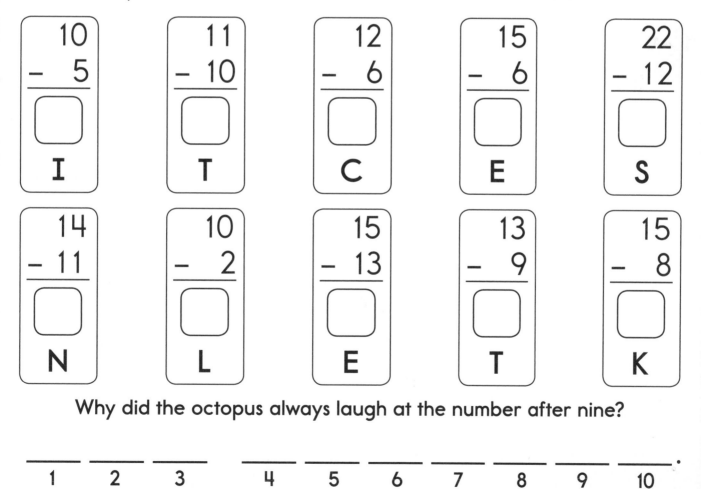

$$10 - 5 = \boxed{}$$ **I**

$$11 - 10 = \boxed{}$$ **T**

$$12 - 6 = \boxed{}$$ **C**

$$15 - 6 = \boxed{}$$ **E**

$$22 - 12 = \boxed{}$$ **S**

$$14 - 11 = \boxed{}$$ **N**

$$10 - 2 = \boxed{}$$ **L**

$$15 - 13 = \boxed{}$$ **E**

$$13 - 9 = \boxed{}$$ **T**

$$15 - 8 = \boxed{}$$ **K**

Why did the octopus always laugh at the number after nine?

___ ___ ___   ___ ___ ___ ___ ___ ___ ___ .
1   2   3   4   5   6   7   8   9   10

Sub Subtraction

START

5 - 4 = ____

7 - 5 = ____

8 - 6 = ____

10 - 7 = ____

9 - 2 = ____

9 - 5 = ____

14 - 8 = ____

8 - 4 = ____

8 - 3 = ____

16 - 8 = ____

15 - 4 = ____

This submarine doesn't know which path will lead it to the ocean floor. Solve these subtraction problems. Then follow the answers from **1** to **15** to get from START to FINISH.

14 - 4 = ___

10 - 2 = ___

15 - 4 = ___

14 - 7 = ___

17 - 4 = ___

12 - 3 = ___

13 - 1 = ___

15 - 5 = ___

17 - 3 = ___

12 - 10 = ___

16 - 1 = ___

13 - 8 = ___

FINISH

Color by the Dozen

Solve these problems. Color in each space that equals **12**. What do you see?

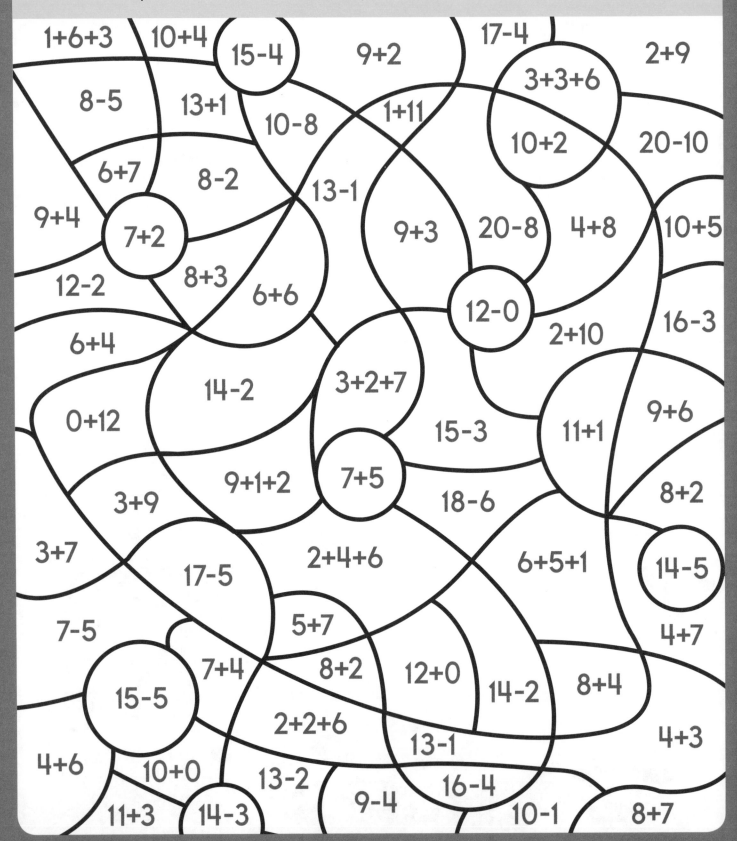

1+6+3   10+4   15-4   9+2   17-4   2+9

8-5   13+1   10-8   1+11   3+3+6

6+7   8-2   13-1   1+11   10+2   20-10

9+4   7+2   13-1   9+3   20-8   4+8   10+5

12-2   8+3   6+6   12-0

6+4   14-2   3+2+7   2+10   16-3

0+12   15-3   11+1   9+6

9+1+2   7+5   18-6   8+2

3+9

3+7   17-5   2+4+6   6+5+1   14-5

7-5   5+7   4+7

15-5   7+4   8+2   12+0   14-2   8+4

2+2+6   4+3

4+6   10+0   13-2   13-1   16-4

11+3   14-3   9-4   10-1   8+7

200

Treasure Hunt

Can you find a path to the buried treasure? Start at the **5** in the top corner. You may move to a new box by **adding 5** or by **subtracting 3**. Move up, down, left, or right.

START

5	10	17	10	7	12
5	7	12	13	4	9
11	6	9	8	21	18
18	19	6	11	16	15
13	18	20	12	21	12
10	15	17	15	20	17

FINISH

Time for Bed

START

$3 + 10 =$ ___

$5 + 7 =$ ___

$9 + 5 =$ ___

$5 + 6 =$ ___

$8 + 2 =$ ___

$2 + 10 =$ ___

$7 + 8 =$ ___

$8 + 5 =$ ___

$9 + 5 =$ ___

$7 + 3 =$ ___

$8 + 4 =$ ___

$7 + 7 =$ ___

$6 + 6 =$ ___

$1 + 9 =$ ___

$5 + 5 =$ ___

Koalas have some odd sleeping habits. They can sleep up to 18 hours a day. Solve these problems. Then help this koala follow the odd answers to his bed.

3 + 5 = ____

2 + 6 = ____

5 + 3 = ____

4 + 5 = ____

8 + 3 = ____

4 + 6 = ____

9 + 2 = ____

8 + 2 = ____

9 + 4 = ____

3 + 6 = ____

7 + 6 = ____

FINISH

9 + 1 = ____

5 + 7 = ____

6 + 8 = ____

9 + 3 = ____

Math Maze

10-9=

1+1=

17-14=

17+7=

22+7=

31-1=

29+8=

28+7=

15-11=

2+3=

32-2=

34-5=

10+20=

14+12=

11-5=

4+3=

31-2=

22+7=

15+15=

16-8=

Daisy got separated from her herd. Help her solve her problem by solving these problems. Follow the answers in counting order from **1** to **20** to the pasture.

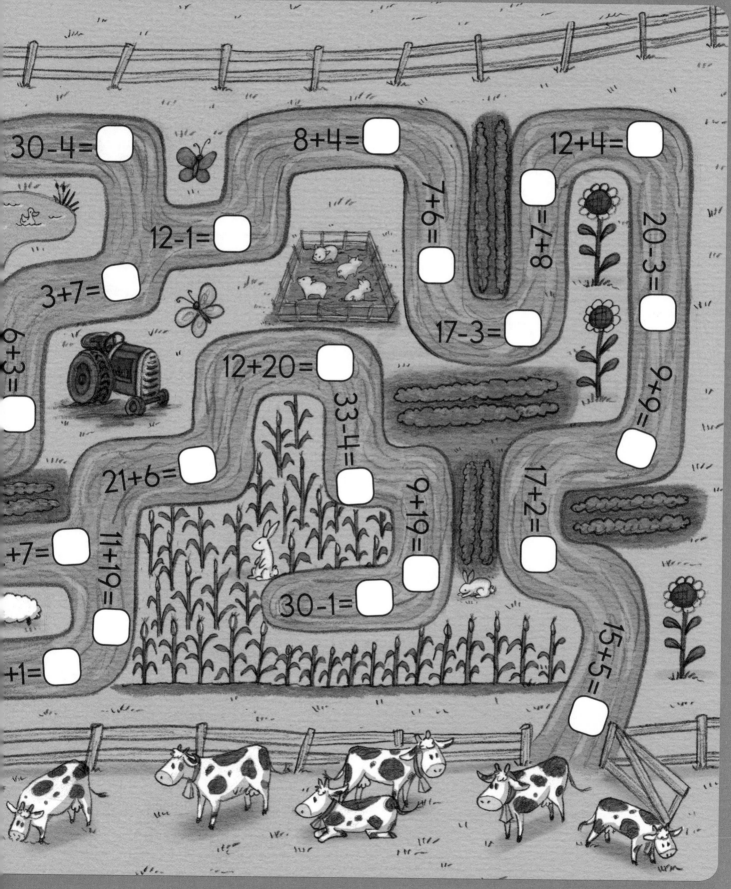

30 – 4 =

8 + 4 =

12 + 4 =

7 + 6 =

8 + 7 =

12 – 1 =

20 – 3 =

3 + 7 =

17 – 3 =

6 + 3 =

12 + 20 =

9 + 9 =

33 – 4 =

21 + 6 =

17 + 2 =

9 + 19 =

+ 7 =

11 + 19 =

30 – 1 =

15 + 5 =

+ 1 =

What Time Is It?

5:10

Write the correct time under each clock.
We did the first one to get you started.

The little hand points to the hour. The big hand points to the minute.

_____

_____

_____

Why did the monster throw the clock out the window?

He wanted to see time fly.

Telling Time

Reginald has to set all the clocks. Can you help him draw the right time onto each one? We did the first one for you,

 2:00

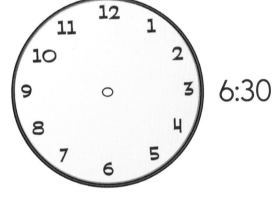 6:30

 7:15

11:10

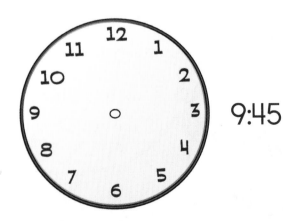 9:45

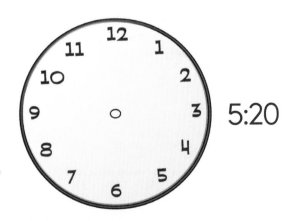 5:20

Got a Minute?

Time for a joke! Read the time on each clock. Then write each clock's letter in the space below that has a matching digital time.

Why was the clock so lonely?

12:00	8:00	5:00	9:45	2:30	6:30	10:50	10:50	6:30	7:45

8:00	10:50	8:00	10:50	3:15	4:05	8:00	10:50

A.M. and P.M.

A.M. is the time between midnight and noon. P.M. is the time between noon and midnight.

Do these pictures show something that's happening in the A.M. or in the P.M.? Circle the correct time of day for each.

Getting sleepy

A.M.   P.M.

Breakfast time

A.M.   P.M.

Good night!

A.M.   P.M.

Getting ready

A.M.   P.M.

Tyler had to be home for lunch at noon, but he got confused about which of his plans took place before noon (A.M.) or after noon (P.M.). Circle the correct time of day for each activity.

Tyler wanted to meet his friends at the park after breakfast.

A.M.   P.M.

Before lunch, Tyler and Erica promised to help Tanya find her bike.

A.M.   P.M.

Tyler had to wash the dishes with his sister Tracy before bed.

A.M.   P.M.

Tyler wanted to build a rocket with Tyrone after lunch.

A.M.   P.M.

Off to the Beach

These pictures are all mixed up. Put them in order. Use 1, 2, 3, and 4 to show the order of the story.

Umbrellas Up!

These pictures are all mixed up. Put them in order. Use **1**, **2**, **3**, **4**, and **5** to show the order of the story.

Making Dinner

These pictures are all mixed up. Put them in order. Use 1, 2, 3, 4, and 5 to show the order of the story.

Art Museum

These pictures are all mixed up. Put them in order. Use **1**, **2**, **3**, **4**, **5**, and **6** to show the order of the story.

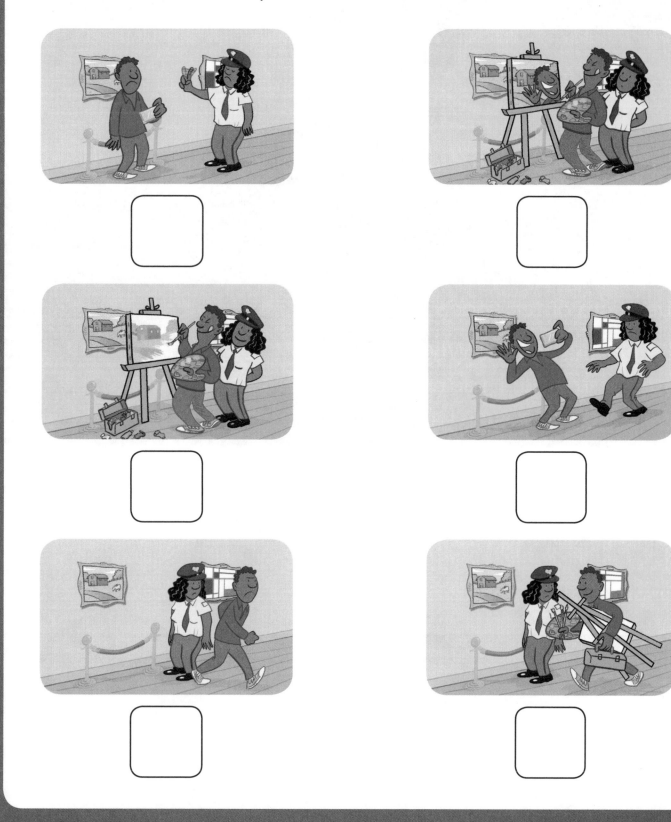

Planet Earth

Earth is the planet we live on.

Earth is mostly made of water. That's why it looks blue from outer space.

The Earth rotates. When Earth rotates, the part facing the sun turns away from the sun. This is how day turns to night.

Find the 2 views of Earth that match.

Outer Space

Find and circle 10 objects in this Hidden Pictures® puzzle.

button · mitten · boomerang · fish · ice-cream cone · pear · yo-yo · wedge of lemon · slice of cheese · heart

The Sun

Read this information about the sun. Then circle the correct word in red to finish each statement.

The sun is a star. The sun gives off light and heat. It is at the center of our solar system. Earth and other planets move around the sun.

The sun is a star / planet.

The sun is at the edge / center of our solar system.

The sun / moon heats the Earth.

You can see the sun from Earth. Draw a picture of it in the sky. Then draw a picture of something you like to do on a sunny day.

Astro Adventure

Help the astronaut get from START to FINISH.

START

BONUS! Are there more blue or red stars?

Venus is the brightest planet in the sky.

Jupiter is the largest planet in our galaxy.

Jupiter is so big that every other planet can fit inside it.

Uranus is tilted so much, it orbits the sun on its side.

What are the clumsiest things in the galaxy?

Falling stars

FINISH

Planet Party

There are 8 planets: Mercury, Venus, Earth, Mars, Jupiter, Saturn, Uranus, and Neptune.

Which planet is the biggest? _____

Which planet is the smallest? _____

Earth

Mercury

Venus

Mars

Jupiter

Saturn

Uranus

Neptune

Find the 8 planet names hidden in this word search. To find them, look down, across, and diagonally. We found **VENUS**. Can you find the rest?

WORD LIST

MERCURY
VENUS
EARTH
MARS
JUPITER
SATURN
URANUS
NEPTUNE

```
L M V E N U S O
J O E E A R T H
U S M R K A F P
P A O A C N L R
I T A P R U U R
T U P L T S R E
E R M O O O N Y
R N E P T U N E
```

Draw a picture below of a planet you'd like to visit. Does it have rings like Saturn, Jupiter, Uranus, and Neptune? Does it have dozens of moons like Jupiter or only one moon like Earth? You decide!

Autumn is get-ready time.
Get ready for winter sleep.

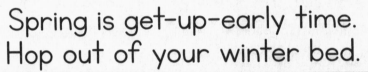

Spring is get-up-early time.
Hop out of your winter bed.

Have a little naptime, earth,
While winter snow is deep.

Get busy, earth, and blossom.
Summer is just ahead!

Weather Words

Label each picture below as one of these four: **windy**, **sunny**, **rainy**, or **snowy**.

_____

_____

Draw clothes you would wear in the snow.

Stormy Weather

Read the poem. Then look out your window. Write your own poem on a separate piece of paper about what you see.

The rain is sweeping by.
The wind is blowing hard.
It must be fun to be a tree
Dancing in the yard!

What's the Weather?

The weather is _____ .

○ rainy   ○ snowy   ○ sunny

horseshoe

ruler

ladder

acorn

How many animals are
playing in the leaves?

○ 3   ○ 4   ○ 5

heart

artist's
brush

sock

Use the pictures to answer the questions. Then find and circle the objects in each Hidden Pictures® puzzle.

The weather is _____ .

○ hot   ○ cold   ○ rainy

ring

drumstick

scissors

teacup

saltshaker

What color is the fox's raincoat?

○ yellow   ○ purple   ○ green

ladle

comb

slice of pizza

Growing Tomatoes

These pictures are all mixed up. Put them in order to show how a tomato plant grows. Use **1**, **2**, **3**, and **4** to show the order.

Off the Vine

Find and circle 14 objects in this Hidden Pictures® puzzle.

party hat · belt · magic wand · pennant · necktie · ruler · teacup · magnet · gift · hockey stick · drinking straw · slipper · T-shirt · mailbox

BASIL

Flower Power

Hummingbirds, bees, and butterflies drink nectar. Nectar is a sugary liquid made by flowers. Help the butterfly, bee, and hummingbird go from **START** to **FINISH**. Which one visits more flowers and drinks more nectar along the way?

Caterpillar Life Cycle

A caterpillar hatches from a tiny egg.

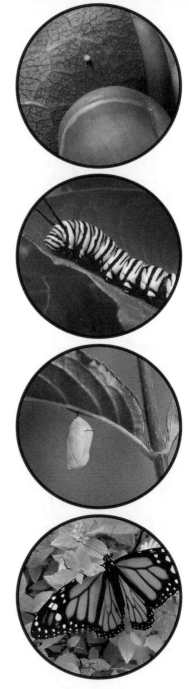

It eats a lot of plants as it grows.

It hangs upside down and builds a chrysalis around itself.

When it is ready, the caterpillar comes out of the chrysalis as a butterfly.

That butterfly lays new eggs.

Use the information above to answer these questions.

1. What does a caterpillar eat?

2. What does a caterpillar build around itself?

3. What does a caterpillar turn into?

Nature Drawing

Find and circle **6** objects in this Hidden Pictures® puzzle.

feather duster   envelope   ice-cream bar   doughnut   flashlight   slice of watermelon

On a blank piece of paper, draw an insect or animal you might see outside.

Living and Nonliving

Things that grow, live, and breathe are living things. Things that are not alive and do not grow or breathe are nonliving things.

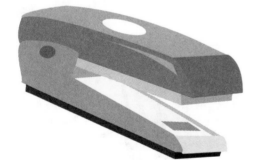

Draw a circle around the pictures that show living things. Draw a rectangle around the pictures that show nonliving things.

Tracks in the Sand

girl

dad

rake

Both living things and nonliving things leave tracks. Match each set of tracks to who or what made them. Then draw a circle around the living things. Draw a rectangle around the nonliving things.

dog

bicycle

sandpiper

Farm Families

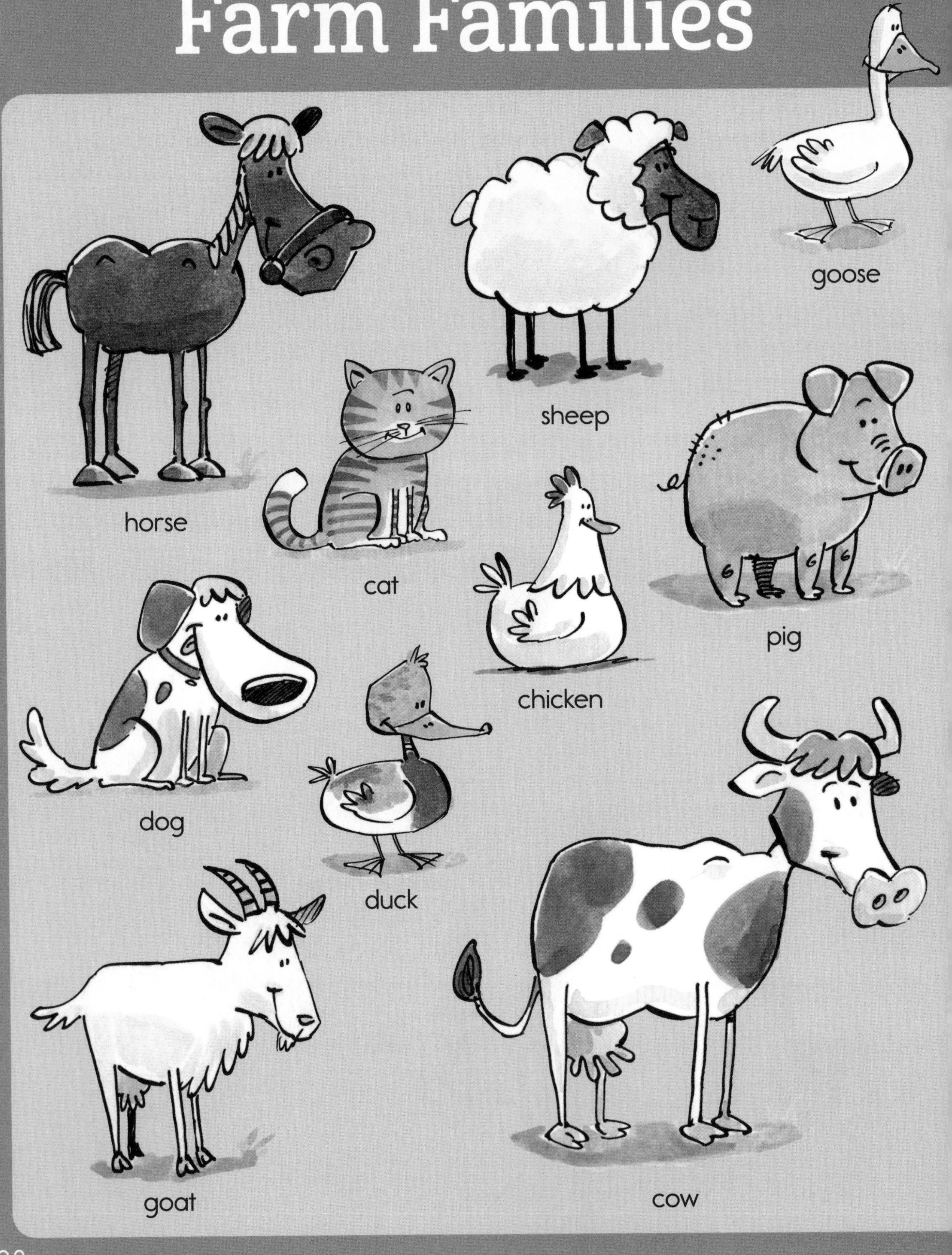

horse

cat

sheep

goose

chicken

pig

dog

duck

goat

cow

Every parent on the left has a baby on the right. Find all 10 matching pairs.

calf

chick

kitten

puppy

gosling

kid

duckling

piglet

lamb

foal

What Sinks or Floats?

1. With an adult's permission, collect some objects.

2. Drop them, one at a time, into a bowl of water.

3. Answer these questions.

   - What sinks?

   - What floats?

   - Did anything float for a while and then sink?

   - What surprised you?

Shadow Shapes

You Need

- Craft sticks
- Foam shapes
- Clear tape
- Flashlight or adjustable reading lamp

1. Place a craft stick on a foam shape. Use clear tape to attach the shape to the stick.

2. Pull down the shades and shine the flashlight or reading lamp onto a blank wall.

3. Hold your puppets between the light source and the wall and make the puppets move!

Look at Shadows

If the sun is behind you, your shadow will be in front of you

The shadows look like the boy, the girl, and the stroller. That's because they stop the sun from shining on the ground.

1

If you face the sun, your shadow will be behind you.

If your side is to the sun, your shadow will be beside you.

And if clouds block the sunlight, you won't have a shadow.

2

3

4

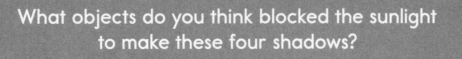

What objects do you think blocked the sunlight to make these four shadows?

243

Sound

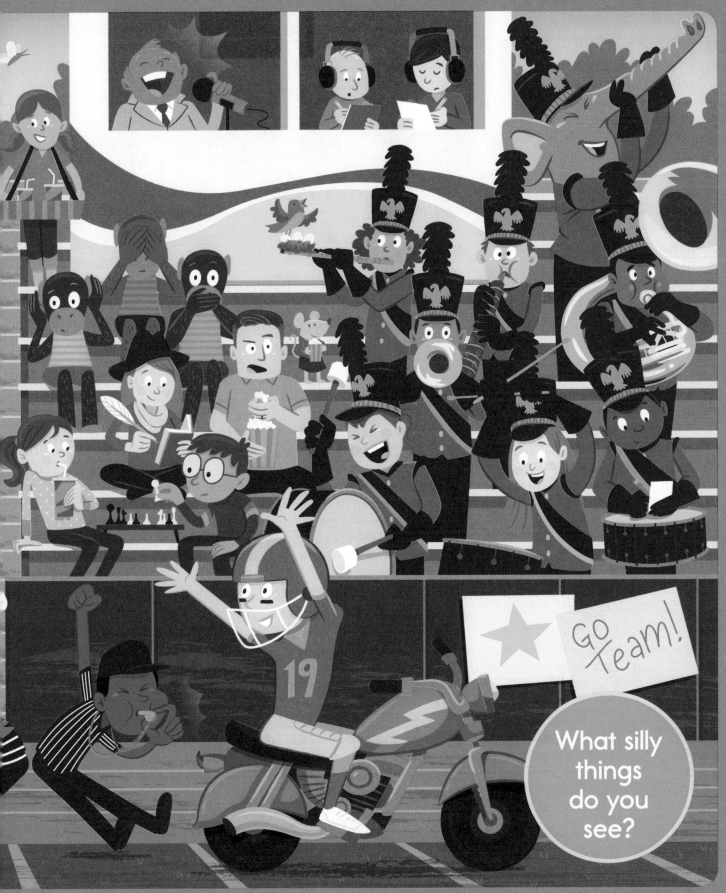

Work Out

Find and circle **13** objects in this Hidden Pictures® puzzle.

balloon

ice-cream cone

button

banana

ruler

paintbrush

needle

ax

teacup

slice of pizza

pencil

anchor

hockey stick

Exercise helps you stay healthy. What do you do to stay active?

Field Day

Find and circle **18** items that appear in the top picture but are missing from the bottom picture.

Scavenger Hunt

This spaceship is one of a few.

A seal on a wheel looks real fun!

This alligator has a short cap and a long cape.

Skip over to count this turtle and his friends.

You can end your search for these scissors with a consonant.

This pig is looking for its baby.

These bluebirds blend right in at the playground.

Her yellow hat is such a bright color!

"B" on the lookout for this bear and his book.

Use the hints to find each of these objects in the book.
What was your favorite puzzle?

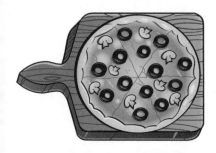

Any way you slice it, that's a whole lot of pizza!

It's too loud to hear this tiny mouse, but you can still find him!

This tree has a-maze-ing apples. Count them 1 to 20.

This lion is LOST at the North Pole.

Why does this planet look familiar? It's our home!

This queen has a question-mark quilt.

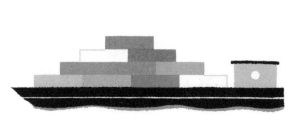

The snowy weather is perfect for sledding.

Set sail to find the shape of these cargo crates.

Got a minute to find this clock?

Answers

Page 11
Bb

```
B A C K P A C K M Q
U B X W B A N A N A
B E E T L E B Z B V
B A N J O M O B A A
L R Q X C Z O R G L
E M B I K E K E E L
W V B A S E B A L O
B O A T B I R D Q O
B U T T E R F L Y N
M W H B U N N Y X N
```

Page 23
Hh

Page 29
Kk

Page 37
Oo

Page 41
Qq

```
            Q U E E N
            U
            I
        Q   L
    S Q U I R T
    Q   E
    U   S
Q U A R T E R
U   S   I
I   H   O
Z       N
```

Page 45
Ss

```
S T R A W B E R R Y
F S S H A D O W Z S
S H A R K S K A T E
A E I S A L A D Z A
N E L N S H O E S L
D P B A X S L E E P
W V O I S O C C E R
I S A L T F J F S X
C X T S M I L E A Q
H S U N X S N O W V
```

Page 47
Tt

Page 53
Ww

Page 57
Yy

Page 59
Zz

```
        B
P U Z Z L E
    U
    Z I P   Z O O
    I     Z E
J A Z Z   B
    Z E R O
    A     A
```

Page 60
Uppercase Letters

What do you call a
lion at the North Pole?

LOST

Page 61
Uppercase Letters

Where do cows go
on vacation?

MOO YORK

Page 62
Lowercase Letters

What did the buffalo say
as his son left for school?

"BISON."

Page 63
Lowercase Letters

What do you call a person
who serves meals
in the ocean?

A WADER

Pages 98–99
Bluebird Playground

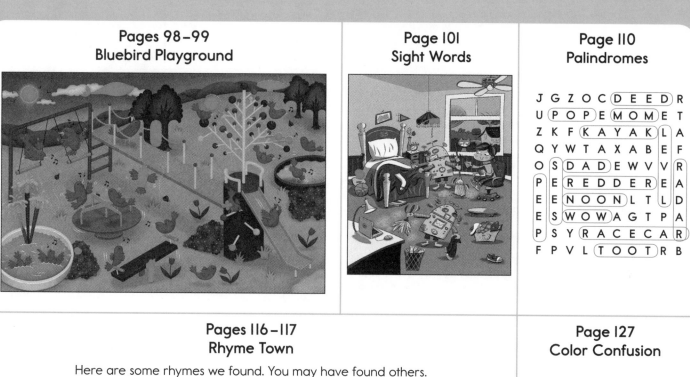

Page 101
Sight Words

Page 110
Palindromes

```
J G Z O C D E E D R
U P O P E M O M E T
Z K F K A Y A K L A
Q Y W T A X A B E F
O S D A D E W V V R
P E R E D D E R E A
E N O O N L T L D
E S W O W A G T P A
P S Y R A C E C A R
F P V L T O O T R B
```

Pages 116–117
Rhyme Town

Here are some rhymes we found. You may have found others.

bat hat	fly pie	owl towel
bear pear	fox box	parrot carrot
bee key	frog log	red sled
big pig	gator waiter	sand hand
book hook	ghost toast	seal wheel
brown gown	green bean	sheep sweep
cone phone	hill drill	snail sail
corn horn	king sing	tree ski
crow bow	lake snake	whale scale
double bubble	moose juice	wide slide

Page 127
Color Confusion

```
R E D G Y E L L O W
M A R O O N Z Z R C
H P B L U E T E A L
V I Z D G R E E N B
I N D I G O Z X G R
O K C P U R P L E O
L A V E N D E R H W
E X O L I V E H C N
T P R X M O G S E W
```

Pages 128–129
A Splash of Color

Page 136
Squares Everywhere

251

Answers

Pages 142–143
Shipshape Aquarium

Page 164
Blooming Humor

What did the dog do after he swallowed a firefly?

HE BARKED WITH DE-LIGHT!

Page 166
Number House

Page 185
Lucky Addition

What's at the end of a rainbow?

THE LETTER W

Page 186
New Neighbors

What do two snakes do after they fight?

THEY HISS AND MAKE UP.

Page 187
Key Problems

What did the pirate get on the test?

A HIGH C

Page 195
Sub-track-tion

What do you call a train with a cold?

A-CHOO CHOO TRAIN

Pages 196–197
Ocean Explorations

Page 197
Ocean Explorations

Why did the octopus always laugh at the number after nine?

TEN TICKLES.

Page 209
Got a Minute?

Why was the clock so lonely?

IT HAD NO ONE TO TOCK TO.

Page 212
Off to the Beach

2

1

4

3

Page 213
Umbrella's Up!

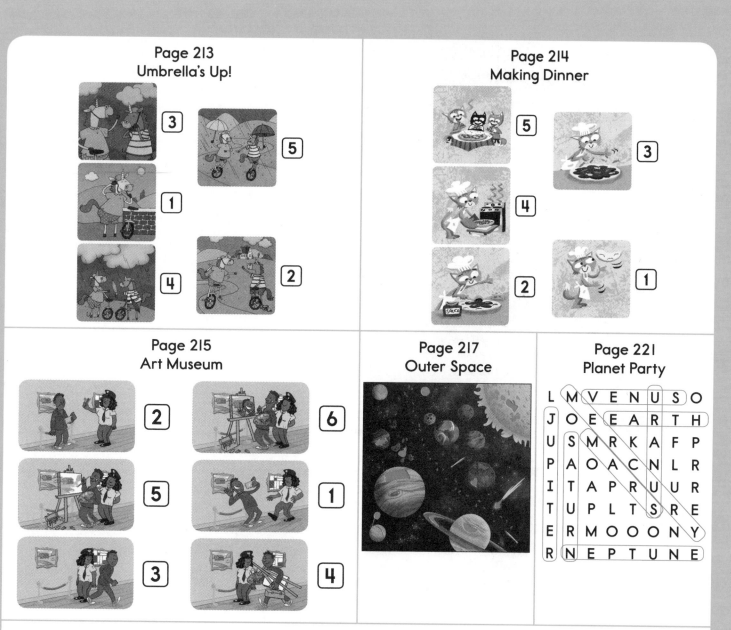

Page 214
Making Dinner

Page 215
Art Museum

Page 217
Outer Space

Page 221
Planet Party

Pages 226–227
What's the Weather?

The weather is snowy.

There are 5 animals playing in the leaves.

The weather is hot.

The fox's raincoat is yellow.

Answers

Page 228
Growing Tomatoes

1

3

4

2

Page 229
Off the Vine

Page 233
Nature Drawing

Pages 242–243
Look at Shadows

1. kite
2. swing
3. bucket
4. bike

Page 246
Work Out

Page 247
Field Day

Pages 248–249
Scavenger Hunt

spaceship: page 169
seal on a wheel: page 117
alligator: page 76
turtle: page 156
scissors: page 87
pig: page 238
bluebirds: page 98
girl: page 129
bear: page 10
pizza: page 175
mouse: page 244
tree: page 204
lion: page 60
Earth: page 216
queen: page 41
sledding raccoon: page 226
ship: page 139
robot clock: page 209

Page 256
Time for School!

Congratulations!

(your name)

worked hard
and finished
The Big Fun

First Grade
Workbook

Time for School!

Find and circle 8 objects in this Hidden Pictures® puzzle.

oar

leaf

pencil

banana

heart

fish

sock

sailboat